# Marilyn Monroe

# Marilyn Monroe

## A LIFE ON FILM
### introduction by DAVID ROBINSON
### compiled and edited by JOHN KOBAL

GONDOLA

HAMLYN

London · New York · Sydney · Toronto

Designed by Dodd and Dodd

First published 1974 by The Hamlyn Publishing Group Limited

First published 1983 as a Hamlyn Gondola Book by
The Hamlyn Publishing Group Limited
London · New York · Sydney · Toronto
Astronaut House, Feltham, Middlesex, England

ISBN 0 600 37310 X

Printed in Hong Kong

# CONTENTS

'Marilyn', wrote Edward Wagenknecht, 'played the best game with the worst hand of anybody I knew.' She inherited a distinctly unpromising patrimony. She never even knew who her father was. He might have been a mechanic called Mortensen, or a man called Gifford who worked at Consolidated Film Industries where Marilyn's mother was a negative cutter, or he might have been a Mr Baker who was the father of her elder brother and sister. Her maternal grandparents were both ultimately committed to mental institutions; her mother, whose photographs show her to have been a woman of considerable beauty, was to spend most of her life in and out of mental hospitals. An uncle committed suicide.

Parental deprivations and childhood penury, oddly enough, are misfortunes that Hollywood's greatest stars have in common. Chaplin's father abandoned the family when Charles was one; Fairbanks' when the future star was four. Mary Pickford's father died when she was four, Valentino's when he was eleven, Garbo's when she was thirteen. Like Marilyn, Chaplin was early deprived of maternal affection by his mother's retreat into madness. Marilyn spent two years in the Los Angeles Orphan Home and the rest of her childhood and adolescence in a series of foster homes. In later years she claimed to have been raped at nine by a boarder in one of these houses; but that may have been a fantasy of her later life, when the person and the role often became confused.

The last of her guardians encouraged her to marry, when she was just sixteen years and three weeks, a 22-year-old neighbour, an aircraft worker who was soon to be drafted into the Marines. Again it is interesting to remark a kind of pattern in the formation of stars: Mae West, Jean Harlow, Rita Hayworth, Betty Grable, Jane Russell, Jayne Mansfield and Raquel Welch were other Hollywood sex-symbols who in private life found themselves physically ripe for marriage before the age of seventeen.

Mae West

Jean Harlow

Betty Grable

What made Marilyn Monroe different from practically all the other great stars was that she was a child of Hollywood, born and reared in the movie capital. She was born on June 1, 1926 in the Los Angeles General Hospital and registered as Norma Jeane Mortensen. (The surname was evidently speculative: the 'e' on Jeane was never used again.) The streets she knew as a child housed the studios, then in their glory, and were trodden by the stars. Even in the orphanage, it is said, her bedroom window looked directly on to the neon sign of RKO.

She was born into Coolidge's American miracle, which in three years more was to end in ruin, but for the moment had accustomed the American people to confidence in material plenty, in cars and radios, ice boxes and women's emancipation, the Charleston and jazz babies, petting parties and Dancing Mothers, speakeasies and gang warfare. Around the time of her birth Dempsey was fighting Tunney; Babe Ruth, Bobby Jones and Red Grange were the idols of the nation; and Lindbergh was about to make his most celebrated flight. Norma Jean's crazy grandmother was one of Aimée Semple McPherson's most fanatical fans, and the baby was baptized in the evangelist's Temple. Alongside all the other enthusiasms of the age, everyone went to the movies. John Barrymore and Mary Astor had just made *Don Juan*, the first all-synchronized feature; Fairbanks had made *The Black Pirate* in colour; Keaton *The General*; Garbo *The Torrent*. Lillian Gish and John Gilbert appeared in King Vidor's *La Bohème*. Norma Talmadge, in honour of whom the child Norma Jean was named, had just made *Kiki*, with Ronald Colman. When Norma Jean was six weeks old, Rudolph Valentino died; and the unprecedented demonstrations at his lying-in-state marked the apogee of America's deification of the mute idols of the screen.

When she was herself a star, Marilyn Monroe explained

Rita Hayworth

Marilyn, hair set Gilda fashion by Helen Hunt

Lana Turner

Marilyn Monroe, *The Asphalt Jungle*

why she would never permit 'ghosted' articles to appear over her name. 'I might never see that article' she told Pete Martin, the *Saturday Evening Post* columnist: 'and it might be okayed by somebody in the studio. This is wrong, because when I was a little girl I read signed stories in fan magazines and I believed every word the stars said in them. Then I'd try to model my life after the lives of the stars I read about. If I'm going to have that kind of influence, I want to be sure it's because of something I've actually read or written.' She also told Martin that she 'used to play act all the time. For one thing, it meant I could live in a more interesting world than the one around me.'

Oddly, however, her biographies and interviews provide little evidence of visits to the cinema, nor indicate at what point her own determination to be in pictures was born. Certainly, a settled determination there must have been, to enable this essentially lonely young girl to survive and persist through the long five years of pushing and rejection, optimism and disappointment, before her first film test and the breakthrough to stardom. The first steps in her career look, in retrospect, casual enough. She was working in an aircraft factory when a visiting photographer taking shots for official propaganda publications, remarked on her photogenic potential. He introduced her to an agent, Emmeline Snively, who groomed her and by 1946 had turned her into a successful pin-up model. In one month of that year she appeared on the covers of five magazines. After a smart publicity stunt invoking the name of Howard Hughes, Miss Snively secured Norma Jean a test with 20th Century Fox, the studio for which the bulk of her subsequent work was to be done. Fox's talent scout, the former actor Ben Lyon, immediately saw possibilities in her but advised her to change her name. Monroe was her grandmother's married name; the Marilyn was Lyon's idea, a tribute to his admiration for an earlier star, Marilyn Miller.

| | |
|---|---|
| Beverly Michaels | Jayne Mansfield |
| Sheree North | Joy Lansing, Barbara Nichols |
| Cleo Moore | Mamie Van Doren |

HER CONTEMPORARIES

Kim Novak

Grace Kelly

Marlon Brando

Elizabeth Taylor

James Dean

Audrey Hepburn

She was given a year's contract at $125 a week, received
a measure of grooming, posed for stills which seemed to
appeal satisfactorily to the press, and worked in a couple of
films. Her single line in *Scudda Hoo! Scudda Hay!* was cut
though it is said to turn up again in some television
versions. In *Dangerous Years* she had a bit part as a confused
adolescent; but her contract was not renewed at the end of
the year. It is interesting that although she went back to
modelling to make a living, she continued to keep up with
the classes at the Actor's Lab, for which the studio had
enrolled her. Through a combination of the influence of
Nicholas Schenck, Harry Cohn, the redoubtable head of
Columbia, and Fred Karger, the film's dance director – all
three, it seemed, personal admirers – she was given her
first featured role in a forgotten Columbia musical, *Ladies
of the Chorus* (1948). She also acquired at this time, in
Natasha Lytess, a studio drama coach, the first of the series
of mentors and confidants who were as necessary to her
morale as they were trying to the studios and film-makers
with whom she worked.

She seemed to move without intending unkindness from
protector to protector at this stage of her career. The agent
Johnny Hyde, more than thirty years her senior, fell in love
with her; and before he died had firmly launched her career
by getting her small but showy parts in the Marx Brothers
comedy *Love Happy*; and in *The Asphalt Jungle*, directed by
John Huston, who was also to direct her last finished film.
After the impact of her brief appearance in this film as the
mistress of an ageing gangster (Louis Calhern) her parts got
bigger and bigger. *All About Eve* contains one of the earliest
autobiographical echoes, as George Sanders sends her
wiggling off in the direction of Gregory Ratoff, with the
admonition: 'He's a big producer. Go do yourself a bit of
good.' The film also contains one of the first authentic
Monroisms, ripostes so deceptively artless that they seem
like accidents. 'You know Miss Caswell, of course?' asks

Marilyn Monroe, Marlon Brando

ille, Illinois, never dreamed once swore, "I'll be famous," vengeance. Nor did they dream of the most glamorous women in Monroe. Keep an eye on this two- mething brewing here...

Sanders gracefully. 'No' Bette Davis brutally snaps back. 'That' comes back Marilyn with sweet and guileless logic, 'is because we never met.'

The roles that followed confirmed her standing as a sex bomb-shell: accustomed the public to the splendid physique (in those days it sometimes tended to sturdiness), the amazing contours clingingly sheathed, the challenging walk which proclaimed her very real sensuous delight in every bit of her body and its appeal, the fresh skin, large, deep, heavy-lidded eyes, and glittering hair. In *Monkey Business* her spelling caused Charles Coburn to cast his rheumy old eyes over her rear and sigh with happy resignation, 'Well *any* stenographer can take *dictation*.' In *We're not Married* she is half of one of five couples who wake up to find that their marriages are not legally solemnized. Undeterred, she transfers her assets from the Mrs America to the Miss America class of the beauty contest. In *Love Nest* her sexual challenge becomes a narrative motive in the comedy itself, an anecdote about a war veteran whose visiting army buddy turns out, to his wife's chagrin, to be a WAC (Marilyn) instead of a doughboy.

It was, though, Henry Hathaway's somewhat irreverent direction of a torrid melodrama of passion, set against the natural drama of Niagara Falls, which ultimately and permanently confirmed Marilyn as a new sex image, more potent than anything that had gone before. The publicity for *Niagara*, showing Monroe spread sensuously and surrealistically across the top of the roaring falls, celebrated the explosive meeting of the old and the new World Wonders. But particularly *Niagara* immortalized 'The Walk', giving her a scene in which, for 70 feet of film she made her way, away from the camera, walking in high heels across cobble stones. 'The Monroe wiggle' was altogether inadequate as a phrase to describe Marilyn's unique ambulation. It was as if her exhilaration in her being and her body exhilarated every part of her (in *The Misfits* Arthur

Miller had her say, as Roslyn, 'You can hear your skin against your clothes' – a remarkable verbalization of pure sensuousness). As she walks it is an undulation, a percussion, a complex independent dancing of her limbs, of her buttocks and the thighs that seem to have an extra curve (she always gave out her *upper* and her *lower* hip measurement). There was never again such an innocently pagan celebration of the zone till Huston filmed her from behind in *The Misfits* as she zestfully accepted a challenge with a bat and ball.

Just before *Niagara* two films had been striking for the autobiographical illuminations which seemed, much more than with any other star, to characterize her roles. Her appearance in *O Henry's Full House* was brief. In 'The Cop and the Anthem' she plays a lovely young prostitute who is accosted by the shabby-genteel old bum played by Charles Laughton. As he walks away she gazes after him and whispers in poignant disbelief: 'He called me a lady!' Several later Monroe heroines would echo the same craving for respect for their own selves. In *Bus Stop* she says, 'I'm going to marry a man that will have some regard for me apart from all that love and stuff.' In *The Misfits* she exclaims to Montgomery Clift with touching delight: 'You took your hat off to me!'

Already Monroe was established as a sex-pot and comedienne; so that her casting as a psychopath girl in *Don't Bother to Knock* was a surprising miscalculation on the part of the studio, earning some of the worst notices of her career from critics caught off guard by seeing the glamour girl called upon to act. Seen in retrospect it is among her most interesting films, and is far from being her least impressive performance. The study of the deeply disturbed girl with her violent changes of mood and her aimless cruelties towards the child she is supposed to be minding must have been painfully close to her experience; and in one extraordinary speech she blurts out bad memories of foster-parents which are strangely like Marilyn's reported

real-life experiences. Much of her playing is artless; but it is undeniably intense and at moments has striking insights.

The scathing notices however taught the studio their lesson. Monroe did not play a serious dramatic role until her very last completed film. After 1953 and *Niagara* her future seemed set and simple. She had arrived and was defined. In what was to prove the last age of Hollywood superstars in the old manner, the decade that also produced Grace Kelly, Audrey Hepburn, Marlon Brando, James Dean, Kim Novak and the grown-up Elizabeth Taylor, Monroe was supreme. Her achievement in establishing a new sexual type was acknowledged by the wave of imitators which followed in her wake.

Because she was a star, and what she was, she defied imitation, just as she defied comparison with other, earlier stars. She was compared with Clara Bow, with whom it is true she shared some qualities of vitality and the personal difficulties; she was compared with Jean Harlow, with whom she shared the characteristics that she was blonde, an archetypal female symbol and uncompromisingly an American image; she was compared with Mae West, with whom she shared a quality of wit, an ability to be sexually provocative while at the same time parodying all notions of sexuality. She can be compared, but she remains unique and herself. Her uncompromising individuality was already evident in embryo long before she became a star, which is perhaps why Columbia, who had Rita Hayworth, and MGM, where Lana Turner was the reigning goddess, both neglected their chance of Marilyn, while even Fox (with Betty Grable) at first seemed hesitant.

The three years between 1953 and 1956, between *Niagara* and *Bus Stop*, were the most serene and unclouded, comparatively, of her entire professional life (and her professional life seems to have become increasingly more real to her than her personal relationships). She recognized *River of No Return*, in which Otto Preminger rather blatantly

Sophia Loren

EVERY COUNTRY SOUGHT ITS OWN MONROE...

Gina Lollobrigida

Martine Carol

Diana Dors

Marilyn Monroe

Anita Ekberg, *Hollywood or Bust*

**FINAL** ★★★★ **M·G·M PRESS BOOK**

**THE WEATHER**
By the U. S. Weather Bureau
RAIN, WARMER TONIGHT. RAIN OR
SNOW, COLDER TOMORROW.

Vol. CVII No. 3,725    **World Wide Coverage of All News Services**    ★ ★ ★ ★ ★   Five Cents

# STEAL MILLION IN "ASPHALT JUNGLE"
## Police Close In On Daring Jewel Gang

Still 1479-57 ... Mat 3-A

### Master-Mind Behind Robbery

Local police are hot on the trail of Doc Erwin Ridenschneider (extreme right), master-mind behind the daring million-dollar jewel robbery at Pelletier and Co. The suicide confession of noted criminal lawyer Alonzo D. Emmerich (left) has also implicated stick-up artist Dix Handley and his girl friend, Doll Conovan, in the robbery. When last seen, Doc was headed for Cleveland, Ohio, in a hired taxi, while police are on the hunt for Handley and his Doll in Kentucky.—Story on page 3.

Still 1479-65 ... Mat 2-F

### Grilled in Jewel Theft

Blonde, baby-faced Angela Phinlay breaks down [————◄] after police questioning regarding her wealthy protector, Alonzo D. Emmerich. At first trying to set up a phony alibi for Emmerich by claiming he had been with her at the time the Pelletier jewel robbery took place, Angela finally admits she lied. A few minutes after her confession, Emmerich shot himself with a revolver.—Story on page 3.

concentrated on her sexual attractions, as a mistake. The series of five comedies made in this period, however, revealed to anyone who had eyes to see that rising above the publicity and the pin-up exploitation she had developed into a comedienne gifted enough to reconcile the constants of a dominating star personality with the individual requirements of quite strongly varied roles. The expansion of her technical achievement in these roles is also striking. In *Gentlemen Prefer Blondes*, happily teamed with Jane Russell, she was a funny and touching Lorelei Lee, who could be poignantly silly or huskily seductive. Her comic reactions were very precise and economical, getting a laugh out of the merest gesture or glance. At the same time she could rise to such knockabout farce as the memorable scene in which, having for some reason become stuck (and small wonder) by her hips while climbing through a tiny cabin window, she conceals her predicament by draping a blanket round her neck. She persuades the infant George 'Foghorn' Winslow to provide legs and arms for the strange elongated figure which results and with which a baffled Charles Coburn flirts ineffectively.

In *How to Marry a Millionaire*, teamed again with actresses of a generation preceding her own, Betty Grable and Lauren Bacall, she lightheartedly undermines her own glamour image, playing some kind of offspring of Betty Boop by Mr Magoo, pop-eyed behind enormous spectacles, and without them crashing recklessly into walls. In *There's No Business Like Show Business*, co-starred with formidable veterans like Ethel Merman, Donald O'Connor and Dan Dailey (in whose chorus line she sang in *Ticket to Tomahawk*), she parodies the convention of the stage musical star. In *The Seven Year Itch* she proves the equal of such a veteran comedian as Tom Ewell, and certainly superior to Billy Wilder's rather heavy-handed comedy. In her first appearance in the film, undulating up the stairs in an astonishingly close-fitting gown, she has to say 'My fan's caught in the door.' She has made her point and is away, while Wilder is still fumbling with close-ups of her rear.

Arguably the finest performance of this happiest period of her career was the 'chantoose' in Joshua Logan's *Bus Stop*. Bravely and pathetically doing battle with her bar-room audience as she gropes her way in a deep Southern accent through 'That Old Black Magic', stumbling on the kick switch which operates the rudimentary lighting effects of her production, or emerging white, blinking and fearful into the daylight, a creature of the night before, this is a complete, authentic and deeply touching character creation.

In certain respects this was the peak of her career. Already the agonizing difficulties which came more and more to dog her working life had begun to torment her – even more than they did the exasperated directors and studios with whom she worked. She had shown herself an independent spirit; and the studios did not expect that sort of demonstration from their dumb blondes. After *There's No Business Like Show Business* she effected the first of her much-publicized disappearances from the Fox lot, rather than accept scripts which she considered did not suit her (and generally, as events proved, with good reason: she had a near faultless judgment of her material and roles). The studio, knowing where their best interest lay, climbed down and gave her *The Seven Year Itch*. After that film she walked out again and settled in New York. The press joined with the studio in their incomprehension that Monroe should really want to be a serious actress. (The sympathetic Pete Martin ironically called his 1956 interview-portrait 'Will Acting Spoil Marilyn Monroe?')

We shall never, of course, know what would have been her future had she not become involved with the Actors' Studio; with Lee Strasberg who endeavoured to supply some of the cultural and professional education which she felt she lacked; with his wife Paula, who was to succeed Natasha Lytess as Marilyn's drama coach; with Arthur

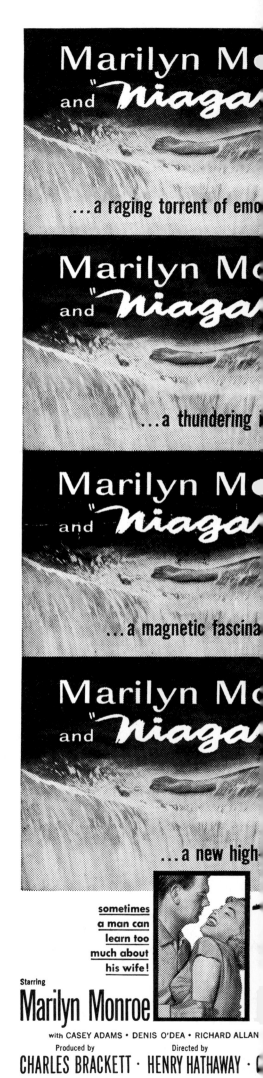

...a raging torrent of emo

...a thundering

...a magnetic fascina

...a new high

sometimes a man can learn too much about his wife!

Starring
**Marilyn Monroe**

with CASEY ADAMS · DENIS O'DEA · RICHARD ALLAN

Produced by                    Directed by
**CHARLES BRACKETT · HENRY HATHAWAY ·**

even nature can't control!

taut excitement!

ng a man to murder!

rk in suspense!

20th Century-Fox presents

*iagara*

Color by

otten · Jean Peters · Technicolor

LURENE TUTTLE · RUSSELL COLLINS · WILL WRIGHT

Written by

ACKETT, WALTER REISCH and RICHARD BREEN

Miller, who was to become her third husband (a second marriage to the baseball star Joe DiMaggio foundered after less than a year). For Monroe it seemed that even more than self-discovery as an actress, New York was able to offer her the chance to be a person, a woman and an artist in her own right, not merely the sex symbol ('I always thought symbols were things you clashed') and inanimate commercial commodity which the studios sought in her. Her aspirations were admirably fostered when she went to London to star with Laurence Olivier in *The Prince and the Showgirl*, adapted from Terence Rattigan's *The Sleeping Prince*.

The dark years were already claiming her however. Already there was the horrifying dependency on drugs, the capricious moods that were to lead to constant psychiatric attendance and periods in mental clinics which, in view of the heritage of her mother's side of the family, must have been terrifying to her vulnerable spirit. The unpunctuality which had been a joke became a disease and a scourge. Distinguished directors gritted their teeth as she failed to show up on the set for hours and sometimes whole days. She seems till this time to have been irresistibly well-liked by her fellow-workers, but her co-stars now began to dislike her. On Billy Wilder's *Some Like It Hot* Tony Curtis was reported as saying that 'kissing Marilyn Monroe is like kissing Hitler'. 'He only said that', retorted Marilyn with cool insight, 'because I wore prettier dresses than he did.'

*Let's Make Love* was the most insignificant film of her later career (surprisingly, for it was directed by one of Hollywood's best directors and an old hand with stars, George Cukor) though the filming proved comparatively serene since her morale was lifted by an affair with Yves Montand. Finally she struggled through to *The Misfits*, her last completed film, and perhaps the most fraught and unhappy production in cinema history. Marilyn's marriage to Arthur Miller, who was on hand as the writer of the film, had reached a critical point. She was ill, frequently

incapacitated by narcotics, and hospitalized in the course of a production which dragged on and on. The unit was divided by factions, bitterness, recriminations. Even John Huston's superhuman patience was tried. The film's fatality seemed to outlast the production. Days after the end of filming, Clark Gable died; and three of the other four main stars, Montgomery Clift, Thelma Ritter and Marilyn Monroe herself were dead within a few years.

She was to make one more effort. She owed Fox a last film on her contract, and returned to the studio where her career had begun, to work on *Something's Got to Give*, again directed by Cukor. In the first month of shooting she appeared for work only twelve times. 20th Century Fox fired her and instituted a suit for compensation. Seven weeks later Marilyn Monroe was dead, killed by the drugs that her psychiatrists prodigally handed out to her to help her chronic insomnia (one of a number of aspects which her career had in common with that of an earlier star and sex symbol, Clara Bow). She was alone when she died; and the body which had once been the most desired and desirable in the world lay for days in the Los Angeles Country Morgue, with no friend to claim it.

What was most striking about these last terrible years, however, is that the more tormented Marilyn's private and professional existence became, the more remarkable was her work and appearance on the screen. As Roslyn in *The Misfits*, it is true a certain quality of the earlier years is missing: the gift she had for projecting a unique and incomparable elation appears only fitfully, though it surfaces notably in that exhilarating scene of the contest with the bat and ball. But there are rich compensations. She has become an actress of depth and sublety and power which transcends a role which is not fully realized in the writing. Arthur Miller clearly based Roslyn on a portrait of Marilyn herself; and was perhaps defeated by his own incomprehension of a girl who is finally incomprehensible to

Marilyn poses for the camera between scenes for *Some Like It Hot*

everyone, including herself. Still there are exchanges which are vivid insights into her personality. Clark Gable tells her: 'You're the saddest girl I ever saw.' She replies: 'You're the first man who ever said that. They usually tell me how happy I am.' Again Roslyn's horror, misery and outburst at the inhumanity of the men to the mustangs is based on the extreme, even neurotic and certainly empathetic sensibility which Marilyn showed in respect of animals; and her playing of these scenes is electrifying. Huston shot the film in sequence; in the later scenes, including these, her physical state shows; but the slightly puffy face, the undue hesitancy of the gestures impairs nothing of the performance. In the film's early scenes she was evidently comparatively well and confident. Leaner, refined maturity gave a new beauty to her looks.

In the few brief sequences that were filmed for *Something's Got to Give*, her metamorphosis seems complete. There is no trace now of the eager, round-faced little pin-up of ten years before, in this woman of breathtaking grace and beauty and luminosity and harrowing fragility – ethereal, magical, haunting. In a series of costume tests she walks and walks again (floating now, rather than undulating), moves her head, repeats the action with that hieratic, ritual magic peculiar to mute rushes; and the result is among the most extraordinary material that the screen possesses. The figure has a presence much more real or immediate than can be explained by the physical phenomenon of a light-painted picture. There seems something supernatural, an independent presence, a being.

It is as if Marilyn had finally accomplished some mystical transubstantiation, translation to another element. It is as if, while her sad mother and grandparents had retreated from reality into madness, *she* had sought to protect her too vulnerable spirit by taking it away, giving it sanctuary, finally, in the screen image. Throughout the last years – all the time that she seemed less and less able to communicate

her fears and doubts and anxieties to those around her; as
she more and more obscured her consciousness with drugs
(years before Billy Wilder had said she 'lived behind a fuzz
curtain'); as people in the street came no longer to recognize
her in the weary and insignificant girl – the screen image
became more real and alive. Gilbert Seldes wrote of Disney
that his creations acquired a special spiritual existence
because they were drawn, practically, on to the film.
Marilyn's image, too, as it appears in *Something's Got to Give*,
seems to be created directly on the screen, as if there were
no mechanical interposition of cameras and cutting and
technicians.

This is all fancy, perhaps: the fact remains that the
surviving enchantment of her screen performances is the
ability, given to very few of the great personalities of the
cinema, to leave on the film the imprint of a real and
complete being. Laurence Olivier said of this being that it
was able to convey 'naughtiness and innocence at the same
time'. She is the most provocative thing that ever was,
flaunting all her considerable sexual possibilities, her parted
lips at once inviting, taunting, on the edge of laughter; yet
at the same time she is as defenceless as a child, with no
more nor less than a child's guile. The sexuality is frank and
open and unashamed. 'Sex is a part of nature and I get
along with nature.' 'Men seem to enjoy me.'

Perhaps her intense sexual allure lay to a large extent in
her pure, uninhibited, exhilarated sensuousness. She had a
delight – quite distinct from narcissism – in her own being
and her body. 'I'm very definitely a woman and I enjoy it.'
She wore her dresses two sizes too small, so that she was
always conscious, from their clinging, of every part of her
physique. ('To wear a dress like that', says an admiring rival
in *Niagara*, 'you've got to start laying plans about thirteen').
She liked to look at herself in the mirror; and it was often
said with malice that the reason for her incorrigible
unpunctuality was her inability to tear herself from

contemplation of her own reflection. Whether she moves or stands or sits, you feel that she is unconsciously feeling and testing and enjoying every limb and every nerve. The nude bathing scene from *Something's Got to Give* is an astonishing moment of exaltation, a solitary act of devotion.

All this was, certainly, natural to her and instinctive. 'I sit down the way I feel.' 'I learned to walk as a baby and I haven't had a lesson since.' 'I use walking to get around.' But the intense joy in her physical being generated an elation which is the irresistible source of her charm, certainly in her earlier roles. In *The Misfits* Gaye tells her: 'You have the gift of life. The rest of us are just looking for a place to hide.' By this time the gift was ebbing, and Marilyn herself had hidden; but still we take this reassurance from her screen presence. Perhaps no one could project so much vitality for so long without finally paying the price, just as Clara Bow had paid for all the spiritual intoxication she had given to the twenties.

But the quality of Marilyn's vitality and exhilaration, certainly in the films of her maturity, was not at all that of a Clara Bow. It was not a brash and bouncing energy. Indeed her special quality is that the joy and elation are always held tremulous on the edge of a precipice of doubt, fear and extreme vulnerability. It is exhilaration always in suspense, fatalistic, trembling lest the next moment it may be wounded. Even when she was at her most sexually aggressive, most triumphant, you never lost sight of the tender, fragile, frightened little thing under the skin, like a Phil May urchin wearing her mother's Sunday boots and hat.

Physically she was obvious, overstated; but her spirit was elusive. Perhaps it was not hard for her to remain so, because her private being defied comprehension – and this was the source of her continuing anguish. There are innumerable records of what she said; few of what she thought. The whole quality of the celebrated Monroe *dicta* is that they too are finally elusive, apparently simple

George Cukor, Marilyn Monroe

Marilyn Monroe, *Something's Got To Give*

and naive, but always suggesting something more or less than the words themselves, some extra significance which is never quite penetrable. Here again the private person ('person' was one of her own favourite words) and the screen image become indistinguishable. From that first worsting of Davis in *All About Eve*, her scripts are never without authentic Monroisms. Did she contribute them or suggest them; or was it simply the way she transformed words by her delivery? Sometimes she seemed to have absorbed and metamorphosed notions from the films. One of her most famous sayings was when she replied, not without mild affront, to a columnist who asked her if she was having an affair with Arthur Miller: 'How could I?' she asked, bewildered; 'He's a married man.' Years earlier, in *The Seven Year Itch* she had used the same logic of innocence when Tom Ewell asked if she was shocked that he was married: of course not, she exclaims: 'I wouldn't be lying on the floor with a married man in the middle of the night if he wasn't married!'

Even if her off-screen sayings were suggested by her roles, the body of epigram and riposte is far too consistent over far too long a period to be entirely attributed to scenarists or press agents (never very witty people). However it came into being, the characteristic mixture of childish sense, acute wit and poetic irrationality are part of the person.

There is so much about her that cannot be explained entirely; and would perhaps never have been explained, even if she had survived to enjoy her person and explore her personality. Though, of course, she *has* survived; or at least that part of her spirit which as time went on was all that really counted for her.

'I'm not interested in money' she told a surprised producer early in her career. 'I just want to be wonderful.' So that despite all the anguish (or because of it) in the end her destiny and her desire came together.

DAVID ROBINSON

# BEFORE HOLLYWOOD CARED . . .

Marilyn in 1945

Norma Jean Baker, who grew up in orphanages and foster homes when her mother was taken away to the State Mental Hospital for recurring losses of sanity, was like millions of other unhappy kids, though her background gave her a head start. She had an all-consuming dream that would solve all other problems: Get into movies! Become a star! Be loved – as she herself loved the stars she went to see. Norma Jean was a chronic movie addict, and being born and brought up in and around Los Angeles fed the dream.

Marilyn, an official portrait for *All About Eve*

What set Norma Jean apart from the millions and led to her metamorphosis into Marilyn Monroe, was her determination to make her fantasy life into reality. Her body was to become her fortune and she showed it off in tight sweaters and skirts. Modelling followed as a matter of course. So did marriage. But by the time she had become a starlet in ermine bikinis, she was single again.

A 1948 publicity shot for *Love Happy*

Robert Karnes, Colleen Townsend, Marilyn Monroe in a scene cut from *Scudda Hoo! Scudda Hay!*

The step from cover girl to starlet is not a big one. She made her first appearance in a rural comedy with the unlikely title of *Scudda Hoo! Scudda Hay!*, rowing in a canoe with fellow hopeful Colleen Townsend. Their scenes had been cut from the film when it was released early in 1948, shortly after she had already been seen in a small role in another film, *Dangerous Years*. Both films were made during her short term contract to 20th Century Fox, the studio whose greatest star she was to become a few years later.

Marilyn between Dickie Moore and Scotty Beckett in *Dangerous Years*

SMW-11-30

The films she was making were nearly all as insignificant as her parts in them, but each led to another. For a time she was under contract to Columbia Pictures, home of Hollywood's reigning love goddess, Rita Hayworth, who was about to go off in search of her own happiness yet again. For Marilyn it was an opportunity to take advantage of the studio's facilities for star building – free voice lessons, drama lessons, and a co-starring role with Adele Jergens in one of the company's numerous B-features, *Ladies of the Chorus*. She was already too

Stages in Marilyn's make-up at Columbia

*Ladies of the Chorus. Below:* Adele Jergens, Marilyn Monroe. *Opposite:* Marilyn (front centre)

good to be any good in it. Studio boss Harry Cohn's reaction was to drop her without regret. Meanwhile the make-up department had gone to work on her, ignoring her individual beauty so readily discernible when the platinumed and Gilda-styled hairdo was hidden beneath a towel and the face was freed by coldcream from the make-up. They saw her as a cheesecake cutie and wrapped her in a cellophane candyfloss mask that could have been stuck to any one of a hundred faces without causing a stir.

The road to stardom can be a long one, filled with wrong turnings and one way streets. To persevere after having been twice tried and dropped, as Marilyn did, demanded an ambition, a need to succeed, that was greater than Hollywood's ability not to give a damn. But then, she had been born in Los Angeles, had grown up in and around the studios, had read the magazines, heard the stories. In short, she knew exactly what she wanted and knew of the struggle it would take to achieve it, and the countless petty humiliations she would be forced to endure. She was young, pretty and ambitious, and the prize, which she never doubted would be hers, would make it all worthwhile.

Marilyn in 1948
Marilyn in 1950

Like Hayworth and Harlow, and like Clara Bow before them, Marilyn had flesh you felt you could touch when she appeared on the screen. When she stumbled into the office of private eye Groucho Marx in *Love Happy* (1948), as a blonde with a dress too tight and a mouth too loose, and told him with an anxious look 'Some men are following me,' it did not need the customary Groucho leer to emphasize how special she was. Though most prospective employers still saw her as prime ogle flesh, the face in the portrait has begun to develop a look of its own, even if it is not yet the authentic finished Monroe.

Marilyn Monroe (right), *Ticket to Tomahawk*

In the chorus of *Ticket to Tomahawk* (1950), an amiable musical set in the Wild West starring Dan Dailey and Anne Baxter, released before *The Asphalt Jungle* and *All About Eve*, she stands out from the rest of the troupe, although the part is little more than scenery. After a mere two years, the girl who had been like millions of others had become the one in a million. Her figure, 38-25-37, had been translated into every language, and each new rival who popped up in her wake had her measurements compared with Marilyn's. Her bright confident smile was seen on billboards and in advertisements for everything in which her studio had an interest. Monthly the glossy magazines vied for attention with articles, photo-spreads and in-depth coverage on her. Nothing could dim her lustre. A publicity man's gag that Marilyn would look good in anything resulted in her posing in a converted potato sack. It was the sort of light-hearted good-humoured lark through which she won ever increasing audiences.

Posed by MARILYN MONROE

Golden Dreams

The famous calendar 'Golden Dreams'

In the summer of 1949 Monroe posed nude for photographer Tom Kelley who needed a 'Golden Dream' girl for a calendar. The calendar went on its regular rounds without creating any fuss, and if she had not made good no more would have been heard about it. In 1952, when she was the world's favourite pin-up, the old calendar was dug out for the sort of publicity that might have ruined her hard-won career. She was questioned about it. Why did she do it? 'Hunger.' What did she have on? 'The radio.' Honesty and humour were her unbeatable weapons.

Monroe was also rumoured to have made several soft-core pornographic films like *The Girl, the Coke and the Apple*, from which these frames were taken. Though blurred, one need only look at the eyes and the shape of the eyebrows and compare them with other images of the early Monroe to see the difference.

Unidentified stripper – probably Candy Barr – in *The Girl, the Coke and the Apple*, c. 1948

A small-budget film directed by John Huston, who was so important in Hollywood that he was even allowed to make small-budget films, proved to be Marilyn's springboard to fame. Her scenes were few but Huston helped her make them telling. Perhaps he sympathized with her aspirations or was touched by her need for approval. More probably he wanted his film to be all of a piece and for that she must be good.

Because she was the only glamour in a film that avoided it, the promotion for the film concentrated on emphasizing her face and body in all the advertisements. For once audiences, usually annoyed by similar con-tricks to bring them into the cinemas, were not disappointed. The film, *The Asphalt Jungle*, was good, and Marilyn came over well. The starlet with the body became the girl with a face and a name to remember. She was on her way.

Glamour shot, 1950

John Huston, Marilyn Monroe on the set of
*The Asphalt Jungle*

Louis Calhern, Marilyn Monroe on the set of
*The Asphalt Jungle*, and *below*, the result

## HOME BUT NOT DRY . . .

Her guileless beauty and unshakeable confidence in her future were qualities to which the camera responded. Her energy commanded attention, particularly among the studio people who make it their business to recognize talent. In company with Bette Davis and George Sanders in the high-powered, prestigious *All About Eve*, she was Miss Caswell, a graduate of the Copacabana School of Dramatic Art – the archetypal piece of 'ogle flesh'. While the high-powered stars prowled through exits and entrances exuding virtuosity, emitting powerful

Marilyn Monroe, James Brown, Mickey Rooney, *The Fireball*

Bette Davis, Marilyn Monroe, George Sanders, *All About Eve*

Dick Powell, Marilyn Monroe, *Right Cross*

Alan Hale Jr, Marilyn Monroe, *Home Town Story*

Starlets were expected to provide their own wardrobe. This outfit also served Marilyn in *The Fireball* (see page 58)

Marilyn Monroe, *As Young As You Feel*

charges of personality and exchanging the sharpest dialogue heard from the screen for a long time, Marilyn played a pretty girl who said little, pushed no one, and wasn't out to do anybody in. She stood decoratively in a pretty dress and smiled disarmingly while the others made asides about her. She was like a tranquil lull in the action. She did not come on as the brash and noisy piece of nightclub glitter the part suggested. She was fresh, and she was noticed.

Marilyn and a cameraman on the set of *Clash by Night*

Marilyn Monroe and David Wayne at a party

Marilyn Monroe, David Wayne, *We're Not Married*

Other parts were offered in a steady stream. The studio wanted to benefit from the public's rapidly growing interest in her. A re-issue of *Love Happy* boasted the legend on cinema hoardings: 'with MARILYN MONROE, that girl from *Asphalt Jungle*.' Metro Goldwyn Mayer, who had hesitated in signing her, not wishing to offend their resident blonde star Lana Turner, saw 20th Century Fox sign Marilyn to a seven-year contract in October, 1950. Although at first there was no noticeable improvement in the quality of her roles, she was on the screen for longer and longer. Stardom was only a matter of months away. Now other studios were making offers for her services and

Publicity for *Clash By Night* (*left*), and with Keith Andes in the film (*right*)

Marilyn Monroe, *Don't Bother To Knock*

Marilyn Monroe being directed by Roy Ward Baker in *Don't Bother to Knock*

one of the few Fox accepted was a significant co-starring role over at RKO – Fritz Lang's *Clash By Night*. She was in prestigious company – Barbara Stanwyck, Paul Douglas and Robert Ryan. Lang, brilliant, professional, was not enthusiastic about the girl whose insecurities in her work created delays. He re-arranged the shooting schedule so no day would begin with any of her scenes. But his star, Barbara Stanwyck, who was not known as 'The Lady' for nothing, told him: 'Don't fool yourself. This girl is a coming star.' She showed neither impatience nor temperament when one of her scenes was repeatedly ruined by Marilyn's difficulty in timing and remembering her few lines.

When the press came on the set, ostensibly to interview Miss Stanwyck, they said, 'We don't want to speak with her. We know everything about her. We want to talk with the girl with the big tits.'* When the film came out Monroe received the attention.

This was the look, provocative, mocking, sensual, which dominated the early 50s and was imitated but never equalled.

* From a letter from Lang to the author

Early pin-up shots

She was gaining praise as a comedienne, and was
loved in and for everything. Having her appendix
out was a cause for headlines and a flood of fan-mail.
She was now the studio's single most valuable
property and earning 750 dollars a week.

Marilyn Monroe, Cary Grant, *Monkey Business*

Recovering from the appendix operation

Alan Ladd, Fred Samris, Dick Powell, Marilyn

Paul Douglas, Marilyn

At the year's end she was a regular recipient of awards voting her the public's favourite. She arrived to collect them with escorts the studio lined up for her, and in dresses they loaned her for the occasion. Like Cinderella she would arrive at the studio before the event to be made up and fitted out: the dazzling, recklessly beautiful package was then driven to the party, where photographers had been waiting for just this moment. Overnight she was the brightest star in that whole vanished galaxy. Outraged by what she thought of Marilyn's image when she had

come to accept the Photoplay Gold Medal award as 1952's most popular star, Joan Crawford, a self-made legend in her own right, lashed out in print at her. Marilyn was not taken aback for long. The news was brought to her on the set of her film by a bevy of journalists, who, hoping for fire or tears, asked her what she was planning to do in return. Smilingly she said, 'Turn the other cheek.'

By now, Marilyn's catchy quips were becoming as popular as photos of her. The studio set their publicity folk to start making them up, but the best came from her and were original.

A publicity stunt

*Niagara* was the first of Marilyn's starring films. There was no longer any question of why people went to movies. She was mightier than the dreaded TV. The kind of out and out man-killer she was asked to portray in the film, wearing suits and dresses fitted so tightly as to make every walk a miracle, was not right for Marilyn. As high tension drama it lacked conviction. As quintessential pop art its reputation is ensured by Marilyn seen here posing with the Falls as a less than subtle backdrop for her own charms; for the way-out boldness of her make-up and costumery; and finally, for the 70-foot take of Marilyn walking down a long street in a beige-coloured suit, a modern miracle of the designer's art in that it became like her skin and yet did not split a seam.

At the time of *Niagara*

Marilyn Monroe, *Niagara*

# LET THE GOOD TIMES ROLL . . .

You're a star when you stop looking like all the others and they're all trying to look like you.

Late in 1952 the All-American girl met the All-American boy, baseball great Joe DiMaggio. When he visited her on the set of *Monkey Business* (1952) it started headlines.

Dwight D Eisenhower was the President in America; in England a young Queen was soon to be crowned. The frights and sights of one war had dwindled, thoughts of a new one not yet begun. Things were safe, and on the whole as dull and staid as safe things tend to be.

Marilyn Monroe, Jane Russell, *Gentlemen Prefer Blondes*

But on the horizon was this shining beacon of liberation, Marilyn – Superstar. Her humour, modesty and insecurity had begun to endear her as much to women as to men. They recognized in her a stargazer, acting out fantasies of dressing-up and inviting audiences to share her dreams with her. *Gentlemen Prefer Blondes* marks the climax of the second phase in her career and the beginning of the third. She was home. Not only was she home, she owned the place, and smiling invitingly from the top she seemed to say: 'You see, it is possible. You too

Charles Coburn, Marilyn Monroe, Jane Russell, Norma Varden, Elliot Reid, *Gentlemen Prefer Blondes*

Jane Russell, Marilyn Monroe, *Gentlemen Prefer Blondes*

Marilyn and Jane Russell at Grauman's Chinese Theatre

can make your dreams come true as I have. I've
done it. I'm here. Isn't life wonderful!' She was an
affirmation of the good things. Now she was
fulfilling fantasies faster than she could make them
up. Her movies – *How to Marry a Millionaire, River
of No Return, There's No Business Like Show Business* –
were earning the studio profits which could be

directly attributed to her. For
when you saw her, you felt good.
Good enough in her presence to
ignore the dull, dumb plots which
she was tiring of. Her efforts to
avoid them would soon lead to
her suspension; meanwhile she
did her utmost to overcome them.
She deserved better things than
the re-hash of old vehicles that
Darryl F Zanuck tended to

Marilyn Monroe, *How to Marry a Millionaire*

Lauren Bacall, Humphrey Bogart and Marilyn at the première of
*How to Marry a Millionaire*

provide for the studio's blonde stars. If she hadn't
realized this, there were enough hangers-on –
agents, lawyers, doctors, drama coaches – to advise
her of her best interests, in which lay theirs. That's
life. That's being a big movie star. She was the
biggest of all.

Nunnally Johnson and Marilyn at the same première

Clark Gable and Marilyn dancing in November 1954

Every country sought its own Monroe – Gina Lollobrigida was Italy's; Martine Carol was France's, and England had Diana Dors. While in Hollywood, a look-alike seemed to pop out of every studio's can of films – Mamie Van Doren, Cleo Moore, Jayne Mansfield, Sheree North, Barbara Nichols, Joy Lansing. These were only a few of them. But imitation is not only a satisfying form of flattery, it offers absolutely no threat.

Marilyn Monroe, Betty Grable, Lauren Bacall demonstrate the CinemaScope ratio in *How to Marry a Millionaire* and, left, relax in the dressing room between shooting

Marilyn Monroe, *River of No Return*

Robert Mitchum and Marilyn in a publicity shot

Marilyn rests on location

Marilyn, Otto Preminger on location

*Opposite:* Marilyn Monroe in torrid costume for an Irving Berlin standard in *There's No Business Like Show Business*

*There's No Business Like Show Business* was a
tribute to the music of Irving Berlin, who visited
the set during the shooting of Monroe's big number
'Heat Wave'. Jack Cole, a regular on her films by
now, was the choreographer, and Marilyn was
developing as one of the most delightful musical
comedy stars of the decade. To avoid making films
like this one, which she thought a waste of time,
she had already experienced suspension troubles
with her studio. There were precedents in the lives
of earlier love goddesses.

Marilyn Monroe sings 'Heat Wave', *There's No Business Like Show Business*

Irving Berlin and Marilyn on the set

She went on suspension campaigning for better roles (most of her best films were made on loan-out) and for more money. Her salary had not kept pace with her earning power. She knew it, and if the studio would insist on keeping her to the fine print in the contract she had signed when she was eager and grateful enough for any straw, why then, there was always the star's time-honoured method of falling ill in the middle of production and holding up shooting. Naturally the studio tried to make her out to be an ungrateful spoilt child, but the charge did not stick. For one thing, the public knew that it was not the studio who had made Marilyn a star but they. While on suspension, the World's Dream Girl married Joe DiMaggio (on January 14, 1954) and after a brief honeymoon, went on a fast, rousingly successful tour of Korea, entertaining the troops. Her singing, or sometimes her mere presence in a plunging cocktail dress in the freezing cold, drew frantic cheers from the happy GIs. How could the studio claim that she was difficult and hope to find sympathy when she was giving herself so freely and generously? No, the public knew

Marilyn sings to the troops on her Korean tour

that 20th Century Fox was the big bad wolf. It was in the company's interest to get her back to working for them and they capitulated to her demands. One of them was to make the film of the popular Broadway play they had bought for her, *The Seven Year Itch*, which was to be directed by one of Hollywood's ace comedy directors – Billy Wilder. It was to prove to be the apotheosis of the Marilyn audiences had come to love, bringing to a fever pitch the climate of Monroemania that had swept the world.

Victor Moore, Marilyn Monroe, *The Seven Year Itch*

But it was also to prove the beginning of the end of the public image of the happy, uncomplicated Marilyn who had won out against all the odds. Meanwhile, her arrival in New York that September of 1954 created a pandemonium at the airport which anticipated the hysteria of the crazed pop fans to come. Her husband joined her there and from the bright smiles they gave photographers who found them eating out, no one guessed that the marriage was cracking-up.

Tom Ewell, Marilyn Monroe, Robert Strauss in a fantasy sequence
cut from *The Seven Year Itch*

Marilyn dining with Joe DiMaggio in 1954

Marilyn stood over a subway grating outside the
Trans-Lux Theatre on 52nd Street and Lexington
Avenue to shoot the scene that marked the
high-point of her love affair with the public,
thousands of whom thronged around during the
all-night shooting. It also marked the end of her
marriage. Take after take was required, and as the
cool air, set off on cue from under the grating, sent
her skirt swirling about her legs in a positive
explosion of goodwill and joy to all, DiMaggio,
standing among the onlookers, couldn't bear the
way others looked on his wife, and left.

After the completion of the film and the end of
her marriage Marilyn escaped to New York; hid in
the Actors Studio, threw herself into classes there
and helped sell tickets for a benefit performance of
*Baby Doll* in aid of the Studio. Spiteful rumours
emanated from Hollywood to suggest it was all a

Marilyn Monroe, Tom Ewell, *The Seven Year Itch*

Joe DiMaggio and Marilyn at the première

Marilyn with her attorney after the break-up of her marriage to DiMaggio

ploy. They said that she was not a member of those sacred precincts; and made her entrance into the Actors Studio sound more as if she had tried to break into the Convent of the Sacred Heart to become a nun than into a school for actors. However, word

Marilyn and Josh Logan on the set of *Bus Stop*

soon came from the sacred coven that she was there,
personally tutored by the High Priests of Method,
Lee Strasberg and his wife Paula. In later years,
when Paula Strasberg's presence on the sets of
Marilyn's films had become too much for her
directors, the sour joke went, 'There's Method in
her madness.' That was yet to come. Meanwhile
there was Art with a capital A bestowing approval
on Monroe's wish to improve herself. After forming
her own company with photographer Milton
Greene as Vice-President, she returned to her home

studio to star in a property specially prepared to her wishes: William Inge's *Bus Stop*. And was it worth it? Was her public still faithful after the year's absence? She played Cherie, the chantoose in a rodeo town who performs nightly to a roomful of loud and drunken cowpokes out for a good time; Cherie, whose dream of success is to own her own mink coat. She ends up in the arms of a lanky cowpoke for whom she is an angel, and as she snuggles against the weather-beaten leather jacket with the rabbity fur collar which he places over her

Don Murray and Marilyn while shooting *Bus Stop*

Eileen Heckart, Marilyn Monroe, *Bus Stop*

Marilyn Monroe, Don Murray, *Bus Stop*

shoulders to keep her warm, the emotion in her gesture says all there is to be said – she has her mink coat.

Alternately puzzled, woe-begone, knowing, conniving, lost, desperate, lonely, confused and unexpectedly radiant with happiness, Marilyn scored her greatest triumph yet. The critics joined the cheering crowds. The intellectuals began to make her their pin-up *and* she had not lost her hold on the public. It was 1956 and she still had no rivals.

*Above:* Eileen Heckart, Marilyn Monroe and *left:* Marilyn Monroe
*Bus Stop*

Singing 'That Old Black Magic' to a noisy crowd
of cowpokes who couldn't care less about her efforts
to entertain them, Cherie is pleased to discover a
fan in Bo, the lanky cowpoke who has come to make
his fortune at the Rodeo and to find himself an
Angel to take back to his ranch. Marilyn and the
film were an unqualified triumph. The question
now was, 'Where can she go from here?'

Marilyn and Arthur Miller at the wedding

Marilyn accompanying Arthur Miller to Washington where he was to appear before the Senate Investigation Committee

# WHERE DO YOU GO FROM HERE?

Arthur Miller, Laurence Olivier and Marilyn at the London press conference to announce the making of *The Prince and the Showgirl*

Laurence Olivier, Marilyn Monroe, *The Prince and the Showgirl*

Laurence Olivier, Marilyn Monroe, *The Prince and the Showgirl*

Laurence Olivier directs Marilyn and Richard Wattis

The first and only film Marilyn made for her own Company was a piece of Ruritanian fluff for which she went to England with her new playwright husband, Arthur Miller. Her co-star and director was the classically trained Laurence Olivier whose failure to appreciate Marilyn's different approach was to lead to a serious rift between them. But the finished product was hers to walk away with.

Marilyn, Arthur Miller at the Royal Film Show, London, 1956

Jack L Warner, Marilyn, Arthur Miller at a New York première

Marilyn in 1956

Scenes from *Some Like It Hot*. Marilyn Monroe and *left* Tony Curtis, Marilyn Monroe

Arthur Miller, Marilyn and Jack Lemmon on the set of *Some Like It Hot*

R-145-3

Marilyn had contractual obligations on her four-picture deal with her old studio to fulfil and in the lull before the start of *The Misfits* made a decidedly dull musical for them, *Let's Make Love*. It was the Spring of 1960, and besides Marilyn the film boasted a strong cast including the French music-hall star Yves Montand, the English pop-idol Frankie Vaughan, Tony Randall and others. Director George Cukor was at the helm. But even talents of their calibre could not bring to life a musical comedy that was not funny and had songs that were stunningly banal.

Scenes from *Let's Make Love*. Marilyn Monroe in her number 'My Heart Belongs To Daddy'

Marilyn coached by Dance Director Jack Cole for the film *Let's Make Love*

Meanwhile her relationship with her husband had virtually disintegrated. She was, however, completely the star and aware of the rules of the game, and none of this is apparent in the smiling photos released by the studio to the press to announce the production. But the break-up of the marriage was no secret from their friends or, for that matter, from Hollywood. While Miller went off to New York to work on the screenplay for their joint project *The Misfits*, a commitment too far advanced and too important to both him and Marilyn for

Press conference for *Let's Make Love*. Arthur Miller, Simone Signoret, Yves Montand, Marilyn Monroe, Frankie Vaughan

19-188

Yves Montand, Marilyn Monroe, *Let's Make Love*

either to drop, and Yves Montand's wife, the French actress Simone Signoret, had to return to France for an unavoidable prior project, Marilyn fell in love with her romantic leading man, an affair that only added to her personal and now no longer private inner turmoil. Gossip columnists like Hedda Hopper, the bitchy apostles who spread the gospel of glamour in their regular epistles to the faithful, leaked the news of the affair, chiding Marilyn and Montand alternately. Strangely, in the finished film, what sparks there were did not come from the

Director George Cukor (back to camera) discussing a scene with Marilyn

Marilyn Monroe, Tony Randall, *Let's Make Love*

personal chemistry between them, but from the professional one Marilyn had with the brilliant choreographer Jack Cole. While even he could do little with most of the songs, the idea of using a classic standard, Cole Porter's 'My Heart Belongs To Daddy' resulted in one of the most delightful and clever musical numbers to come out of any of Marilyn's films. The film was Marilyn's first failure with her public, even though interest in her and her work had not slackened. On the contrary, few weeks went by when her face was not on the cover of

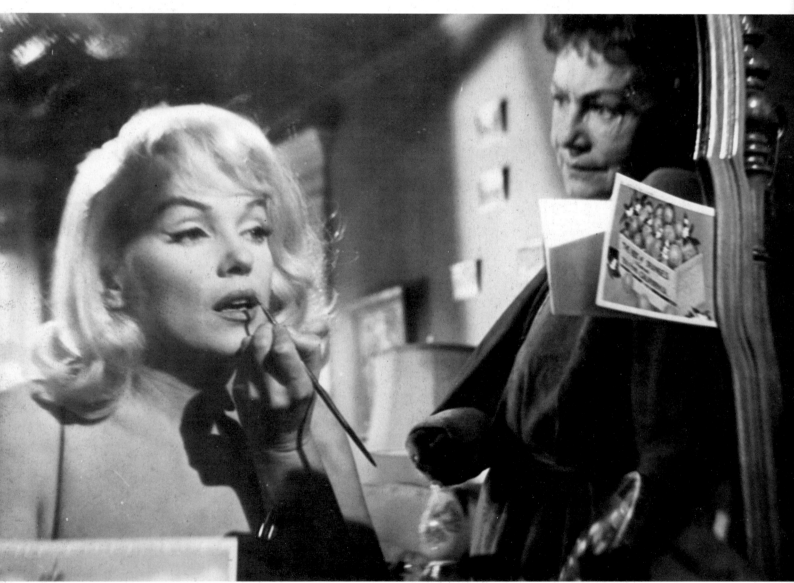

Marilyn Monroe, Thelma Ritter, *The Misfits*

magazines, or when she was not being written up in the press. Like Hayworth, she was one of those people who attract interest without needing to do anything. Her private life, constantly on the front pages, was fuel to the fire. It would all come together for *The Misfits*. The title and idea came from a short story Miller had written several years before, and on her instigation had shaped into a vehicle for his wife. Neither could then have anticipated how time was to alter them and make it tragically reminiscent of their life and her career.

Arthur Miller and Marilyn Monroe pose during the shooting of *The Misfits*

Marilyn on location for *The Misfits*

Marilyn and Montgomery Clift pose for a publicity still for *The Misfits*

Marilyn and a crew member's daughter on location for *The Misfits*

In July 1960, *The Misfits* began shooting in Reno, Nevada. John Huston, who had guided Marilyn through her first significant role, helping to launch her on to the career that made her the most loved star in the world, was chosen to be the director for what would prove to be Marilyn's last film. Clark Gable, 'The King', had been on top of Hollywood's totem pole ever since he slugged and loved the screen's great love goddesses in the 30s. He was the star Norma Jean had dreamed about and idolized; the star Marilyn Monroe had danced with

Marilyn being made-up for *The Misfits*

Director John Huston, Marilyn and Clark Gable at a birthday party during the filming of *The Misfits*

in 1954; the actor who hoped that his part in the film would prove a worthy climax to a memorable career, and who died from a heart attack brought on by the exertions imposed during shooting. The screenplay was Arthur Miller's first. It was written as a tribute to his wife, and it marked the end of their marriage.

Estelle Winwood, Eli Wallach. Montgomery Clift, Marilyn Monroe, Clark Gable, *The Misfits*

Eli Wallach, Montgomery Clift, Marilyn Monroe, Clark Gable, *The Misfits*

Clark Gable, Marilyn Monroe, *The Misfits*. The last scene of the last completed film for either star

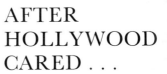

Marilyn with husband Arthur Miller leaving a New York hospital after she had undergone an operation after a miscarriage in 1961

# AFTER HOLLYWOOD CARED . . .

Those whom the Gods love, they destroy. Marilyn went on to begin work on one more film. She seemed to overcome her private problems and encroaching age, to start work on *Something's Got To Give*. She had never looked more beautiful. She seemed, from photographs and tests made for the film, to have become as luminous as the beam of light transferring her image from film to the screen. Her beauty was so fragile, so insubstantial, that it seemed as if like gossamer it would disintegrate at a touch.

Marilyn after her separation from Arthur Miller

Marilyn, Arthur Miller and Eli Wallach on location for *The Misfits*

**Marilyn, Arthur Miller and Eli Wallach on location for**
*The Misfits*

Photographs by Lawrence Schiller of Marilyn Monroe during the filming of *Something's Got To Give*. Marilyn allowed herself to be photographed nude for the first time since the famous calendar shot fifteen years earlier

Marilyn died from a drug overdose.

Much has been rumoured and conjectured about her death.

Circumstances seemed to make it inevitable. From what one knows about her – the fluctuating moods, the ability to revive and regenerate herself after the various crises of her life (compare the plumpish Marilyn of *Let's Make Love* with the radiant creature of *Something's Got to Give*) – one senses that, whatever else it was, her death could not have been deliberate. For years she had been living on pills. Pills to make

Wardrobe shots taken for the film *Something's Got To Give* which were later used in the composite film *Marilyn* made after her death

Marilyn with ex-husband Joe DiMaggio at a baseball
game in 1961

her sleep, pills to wake her, pills to slow her up when
she was too stimulated, pills to tone her down, pills
to overcome pills. The pills eventually weakened her
physical and mental resistance, added to her
confusion, slowed down her reflexes in times of stress
such as those last days must have been. But planned

Marilyn Monroe, *Something's Got To Give*

George Cukor briefs Marilyn during filming of *Something's Got To Give*

Marilyn learns her future from a palmist

Marilyn with Mexican screen writer José Bolanes at an award dinner shortly before her death

death, the deliberate taking of her own life – that is the one conclusion it would be wrong to make. She stood for Life. She radiated Life. In her smile hope was always present. She glorified in Life, and her death did not mar this final image. She had become a legend in her own time, and in her death took her place among the myths of our century.

Marilyn receives an award for being the world's most popular star: soon afterwards she was dead

The body of Marilyn Monroe arriving at the mortuary, August 5, 1962

The crowd approaches the crypt in which the body of Marilyn Monroe was interred to pick flower souvenirs from it

Mrs Bernice Miracle (right), Marilyn's half-sister, clinging to the hand of Inez Nelson, Marilyn's friend and business manager, as they arrive at the Westwood Mortuary to arrange for Marilyn's funeral

The casket of Marilyn Monroe being placed on a stand at Westwood Park Memorial Cemetery.
The curtained crypt on the left is Marilyn's last resting place

# Dangerous Years

### 20th CENTURY FOX 9/12/1947

## CAST

| | |
|---|---|
| DANNY JONES | WILLIAM HALOP |
| DORIS MARTIN | ANN E TODD |
| WILLY MILLER | SCOTTY BECKETT |
| WESTON | JEROME COWAN |
| EVE, A WAITRESS | MARILYN MONROE |
| BURNS, AN ATTORNEY | RICHARD GAINES |
| JEFF CARTER | DONALD CURTIS |
| | (AND ANNABEL SHAW, |
| | DICKIE MOORE) |

## CREDITS

| | |
|---|---|
| DIRECTOR | ARTHUR PIERSON |
| SCREENPLAY AND STORY | ARNOLD BELGARD |
| DIRECTOR OF PHOTOGRAPHY | BENJAMIN KLINE |
| MUSIC | RUDY SCHRAGER |
| EDITOR | FRANK BALRIDGE |
| PRODUCED BY | SOL WURTZEL |

RUNNING TIME 1 HOUR
3 MINS

Donald Curtis, Marilyn

# Scudda Hoo! Scudda Hay!

### LATER KNOWN AS 'SUMMER LIGHTNING'
### 20th CENTURY FOX 4/3/1948

## CAST

| | |
|---|---|
| RAD McGILL | JUNE HAVER |
| SNUG DOMINY | LON McCALLISTER |
| TONY MAULE | WALTER BRENNAN |
| JUDITH DOMINY | ANNE REVERE |
| BEAN McGILL | NATALIE WOOD |
| STRETCH DOMINY | ROBERT KARNES |
| MILT DOMINY | HENRY HULL |
| ROARER McGILL | TOM TULLY |
| CHES | LEE MacGREGOR |
| MRS McGILL | GERALDINE WALL |
| SHERIFF BURSOM | KEN CHRISTY |
| JUDGE STILLWELL | TOM MOORE |
| JIM | MATT McHUGH |
| BARBER | CHARLES WAGENHEIM |
| DUGAN | HERBERT HEYWOOD |
| TED | EDWARD GARGAN |
| ELMER | GUY BEACH |
| MALONE | G PAT COLLINS |
| JEFF | CHARLES WOOLF |
| STABLE HAND | EUGENE JACKSON |
| GIRL FRIENDS | COLLEEN TOWNSEND |
| | MARILYN MONROE |

## CREDITS

| | |
|---|---|
| DIRECTED BY | F HUGH HERBERT |
| PRODUCED BY | WALTER MOROSCO |
| SCREENPLAY BY | F HUGH HERBERT |
| FROM A NOVEL BY | GEORGE AGNEW |
| | CHAMBERLAIN |
| COLOUR BY TECHNICOLOR | |
| TECHNICOLOR COLOUR | |
| DIRECTOR | NATALIE KALMUS |
| ASSOCIATE | LEONARD DOSS |
| DIRECTOR OF PHOTOGRAPHY | ERNEST PALMER, ASC |
| COSTUMES DESIGNED BY | BONNIE CASHIN |
| MUSIC | CYRIL MOCKRIDGE |
| CONDUCTED BY | LIONEL NEWMAN |

LENGTH 8,496 FEET
RUNNING TIME 1 HOUR
35 MINS

# Ladies of the Chorus

COLUMBIA 1949

## CAST

| | |
|---|---|
| MAY MARTIN | ADELE JERGENS |
| PEGGY MARTIN | MARILYN MONROE |
| RANDY CARROLL | RANDY BROOKS |
| MRS CARROLL | NANA BRYANT |
| BILLY MACKAY | EDDIE GARR |
| SALISBURY | STEVEN GERAY |
| ALAN WAKEFIELD | BILL EDWARDS |
| BUBBLES LaRUE | MARJORIE HOSHELLE |
| JOE | FRANK SCANNELL |
| RIPPLE | DAVE BARRY |
| RIPPLE JR | ALAN BARRY |
| TOM LAWSON | MYRON HEALEY |
| PETER WINTHROP | ROBERT CLARKE |
| FLOWER SHOP GIRL | GLADYS BLAKE |
| DOCTOR | EMMETT VOGAN |

## CREDITS

| | |
|---|---|
| SCREENPLAY BY | HARRY SAUBER, JOSEPH CAROLE |
| STORY BY | HARRY SAUBER |
| DIRECTED BY | PHIL KARLSON |
| ASSISTANT DIRECTOR | CARTER DeHAVEN |
| DIRECTOR OF PHOTOGRAPHY | FRANK REDMAN, ASC |
| FILM EDITOR | RICHARD FANTL |
| PRODUCTION NUMBERS STAGED BY | JACK BOYLE |
| MUSICAL SUPERVISOR | FRED KARGER |
| MUSICAL DIRECTOR | MISCHA BAKALEINIKOFF |
| SONGS BY | ALLAN ROBERTS, LESTER LEE |
| UBANGI LOVE SONG BY | BUCK RAM |
| PRODUCED BY | HARRY A ROMM |
| COSTUMES | JEAN-LOUIS |

RUNNING TIME 61 MINS

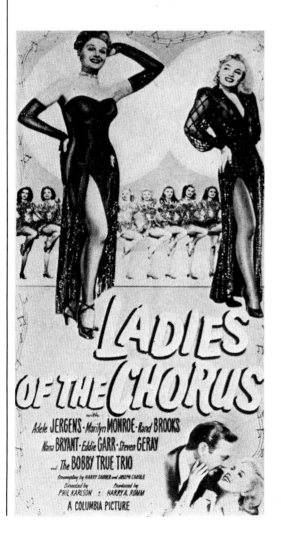

# Love Happy

UA 10/10/1949

## CAST

| | |
|---|---|
| HARPO | HARPO MARX |
| FAUSTINO THE GREAT | CHICO MARX |
| SAM GRUNION | GROUCHO MARX |
| MAGGIE PHILLIPS | VERA-ELLEN |
| MADAME EGILICHI | ILONA MASSEY |
| BUNNY DOLAN | MARION HUTTON |
| ALPHONSO ZOTTO | RAYMOND BURR |
| THROCKMORTON | MELVILLE COOPER |
| MACKINAW | ERIC BLORE |
| HANNIBAL ZOTO | BRUCE GORDON |
| GRUNION'S CLIENT | MARILYN MONROE |

## CREDITS

| | |
|---|---|
| PRODUCER | LESTER COWAN |
| PRESENTED BY | MARY PICKFORD |
| DIRECTOR | DAVID MILLER |
| SCREENPLAY | FRANK TASHLIN, MAC BENOFF |
| FROM A STORY BY | HARPO MARX |
| PHOTOGRAPHY | WILLIAM C MELLOR |
| EDITING | BASIL WRANGELL, AL JOSEPH |
| MUSIC | ANN RONELL |
| ART DIRECTOR | GABRIEL SCOGNAMILLO |

RUNNING TIME 85 MINS

Groucho Marx, Marilyn

# A Ticket to Tomahawk

### 20th CENTURY FOX 21/4/1950

## CAST

| | |
|---|---|
| JOHNNY | DAN DAILEY |
| KIT DODGE JR | ANNE BAXTER |
| DAKOTA | RORY CALHOUN |
| TERENCE SWEENY | WALTER BRENNAN |
| CHUCKITY | CHARLES KEMPER |
| MADAME ADELAIDE | CONNIE GILCHRIST |
| SAD EYES | ARTHUR HUNNICUTT |
| DODGE | WILL WRIGHT |
| PAWNEE | CHIEF YOWLACHIE |
| LONG TIME | VICTOR SEN YUNG |
| DAWSON | MAURITZ HUGO |
| MAYOR | RAYMOND GREENLEAF |
| CHARLEY | HARRY CARTER |
| VELVET FINGERS | HERRY SEYMOUR |
| BAT | ROBERT ADLER |
| GILO | LEE MacGREGOR |
| STATION MASTER | RAYMOND BOND |
| TRANCOS | CHARLIE STEVENS |
| CROOKED KNIFE | CHIEF THUNDERCLOUD |
| ANNIE | MARION MARSHALL |
| RUBY | JOYCE MACKENZIE |
| CLARA | MARILYN MONROE |
| JULIE | BARBARA SMITH |
| FARGO | JACK ELAM |

## CREDITS

| | |
|---|---|
| DIRECTED BY | RICHARD SALE |
| PRODUCED BY | ROBERT BASSLER |
| WRITTEN BY | MARY LOOS & RICHARD SALE |
| COLOUR BY TECHNICOLOR | |
| MUSIC | CYRIL MOCKRIDGE |
| MUSICAL DIRECTION | LIONEL NEWMAN |
| ORCHESTRATION | HERBERT SPENCER, EARLE HAGEN |
| DIRECTOR OF PHOTOGRAPHY | HARRY JACKSON, ASC |
| ART DIRECTION | LYLE WHEELER, GEORGE W DAVIS |
| FILM EDITOR | HARMON JONES |
| COSTUMES DESIGNED BY | RENE HUBERT |
| DANCES STAGED BY | KENNY WILLIAMS |

RUNNING TIME 1 HOUR
31 MINS

Marion Marshall, Joyce MacKenzie, Dan Dailey, Barbara Smith, Marilyn

# The Asphalt Jungle

### MGM 5/5/1950

## CAST

| | |
|---|---|
| DIX HANDLEY | STERLING HAYDEN |
| ALONZO D EMMERICH | LOUIS CALHERN |
| DOLL CONOVAN | JEAN HAGEN |
| GUS MINISSI | JAMES WHITMORE |
| DOC ERWIN RIEDENSCHNEIDER | SAM JAFFE |
| POLICE COMMISSIONER | |
| HARDY | JOHN McINTIRE |
| COBBY | MARC LAWRENCE |
| LT DIETRICH | BARRY KELLY |
| LOUIS CIAVELLI | ANTHONY CARUSO |
| MARIA CIAVELLI | TERESA CELLI |
| ANGELA PHINLAY | MARILYN MONROE |
| MAY EMMERICH | DOROTHY TREE |
| BOB BRANNOM | BRAD DEXTER |

## CREDITS

| | |
|---|---|
| DIRECTOR | JOHN HUSTON |
| SCREENPLAY | JOHN HUSTON, BEN MADDOW |
| FROM A NOVEL BY | W R BURNETT |
| PHOTOGRAPHY | HAROLD ROSSEN |
| MUSIC | MIKLOS ROSZA |
| COSTUMES | HELEN ROSE |
| EDITOR | GEORGE BOEMLER |
| ART DIRECTOR | CEDRIC GIBBONS, RANDALL DVELL |

RUNNING TIME 112 MINS

# The Fireball

20th CENTURY FOX 16/8/1950

## CAST

| | |
|---|---|
| JOHNNY CASAR | MICKEY ROONEY |
| FATHER O'HARA | PAT O'BRIEN |
| MARY REEVES | BEVERLY TYLER |
| MACK MILLER | GLENN CORBETT |
| ALLAN | JAMES BROWN |
| POLLY | MARILYN MONROE |
| NICK | RALPH DUMKE |

## CREDITS

| | |
|---|---|
| PRODUCER | BERT FRIEDLOB |
| DIRECTOR | TAY GARNETT |
| SCREENPLAY | TAY GARNETT, HORACE McCOY |
| MUSIC | VICTOR YOUNG |
| PHOTOGRAPHY | LESTER WHITE |
| FILM EDITOR | FRANK SULLIVAN |
| ART DIRECTOR | VAN NEST POLGLASE |

LENGTH 7,519 FEET
RUNNING TIME 1 HOUR
24 MINS

Just a little Guy...A Punk...but on skates he was a **Flying Demon!**

He was a runt in a man's game...crashing to the top on screaming wheels!

The first picture ever made of America's newest sport craze— roller banked-track racing... the world's most dangerous game!

THOR PRODUCTIONS presents

MICKEY **ROONEY** PAT **O'BRIEN**

in

**The FIREBALL**

Rooney Runs Riot on the Roller Raceways!

with BEVERLY TYLER

JAMES BROWN · MARILYN MONROE · RALPH DUMKE
BERT BEGLEY · MILBURN STONE · SAM FLINT · JOHN HEDLOE
and introducing GLENN CORBETT

Produced by BERT FRIEDLOB · Directed by TAY GARNETT

Screenplay by Tay Garnett and Horace McCoy
A THOR PRODUCTION · Released by 20th Century-Fox

S I G N A T U R E

# All About Eve

20th CENTURY FOX 13/9/1950

## CAST

| | |
|---|---|
| MARGO CHANNING | BETTE DAVIS |
| EVE HARRINGTON | ANNE BAXTER |
| ADDISON DE WITT | GEORGE SANDERS |
| KAREN RICHARDS | CELESTE HOLM |
| BILL SIMPSON | GARY MERRILL |
| LLOYD RICHARDS | HUGH MARLOWE |
| BIRDIE | THELMA RITTER |
| MISS CASSWELL | MARILYN MONROE |
| MAX FABIAN | GREGORY RATOFF |
| PHOEBE | BARBARA BATES |
| ACTOR | WALTER HAMPDEN |
| GIRL | RANDY STUART |
| LEADING MAN | CRAIG HILL |
| CAPTAIN OF THE WAITERS | STEVE GERAY |
| STAGE MANAGER | EDDIE FISHER |

## CREDITS

| | |
|---|---|
| DIRECTED BY | JOSEPH L MANKIEWICZ |
| WRITTEN BY | JOSEPH L MANKIEWICZ |
| BASED ON THE STORY | 'THE WISDOM OF EVE' BY MARY ORR |
| MUSIC | ALFRED NEWMAN |
| PHOTOGRAPHY | MILTON KRASNER |
| EDITOR | BARBARA McLEAN |
| COSTUMES | EDITH HEAD, CHARLES LeMAIRE |

RUNNING TIME 128 MINS

Gregory Ratoff, Anne Baxter, Gary Merrill,
Marilyn Monroe, George Sanders, Celeste Holm

# Right Cross

MGM 22/8/1950

## CAST

| | |
|---|---|
| PAT O'MALLEY | JUNE ALLYSON |
| RICK GAVERY | DICK POWELL |
| JOHNNY MONTEREZ | RICARDO MONTALBAN |
| SEAN O'MALLEY | LIONEL BARRYMORE |
| MARINA MONTEREZ | TERESA CELLI |
| TOM BALFORD | TOM POWERS |
| THIRD REPORTER | KEN TOBEY |
| GIRL IN CLUB | MARILYN MONROE |

## CREDITS

| | |
|---|---|
| DIRECTOR | JOHN STURGES |
| SCRIPT | CHARLES SCHNEE |
| PHOTOGRAPHY | NORBERT BRODINE |
| EDITOR | JAMES E NEWCOM |
| MUSIC | DAVID RASKIN |
| COSTUMES | HELEN ROSE |

RUNNING TIME 89 MINS

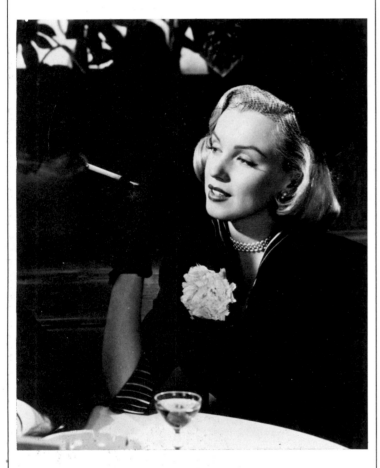

# Home Town Story

MGM 14/5/1951

## CAST

| | |
|---|---|
| LAKE WASHBOURNE | JEFFREY LYNN |
| JOHN McFARLANE | DONALD CRISP |
| JANICE HUNT | MARJORIE REYNOLDS |
| SLIM HASKINS | ALAN HALE JR |
| IRIS MARTIN | MARILYN MONROE |
| MRS WASHBURN | BARBARA BROWN |

## CREDITS

| | |
|---|---|
| DIRECTOR | ARTHUR PIERSON |
| AUTHOR | ARTHUR PIERSON |
| SCREENPLAY | ARTHUR PIERSON |
| PHOTOGRAPHY | LUCIEN ANDRIOT |
| MUSIC | LOUIS FORBES |
| EDITOR | WILLIAM CLAXTON |

RUNNING TIME 61 MINS

Jeffrey Lynn, Marilyn Monroe

# As Young as You Feel

20th CENTURY FOX 13/6/1951

## CAST

| | |
|---|---|
| JOHN HODGES | MONTY WOOLLEY |
| DELLA HODGES | THELMA RITTER |
| JOE | DAVID WAYNE |
| ALICE HODGES | JEAN PETERS |
| LUCILLE McKINLEY | CONSTANCE BENNETT |
| HARRIET | MARILYN MONROE |
| GEORGE HODGES | ALLYN JOSLYN |
| LOUIS McKINLEY | ALBERT DEKKER |
| FRANK ERICKSON | CLINTON SUNDBERG |
| CLEVELAND | MINOR WATSON |
| CONDUCTOR | LUDWIG STOSSEL |
| HARPIST | RENIE RIANO |
| GALLAGHER | WALLY BROWN |
| WILLIE | RUSTY TAMBLYN |
| SALTONSTALL | ROGER MOORE |

## CREDITS

| | |
|---|---|
| PRODUCED BY | LAMAR TROTTI |
| DIRECTED BY | HARMON JONES |
| SCREENPLAY BY | LAMAR TROTTI |
| BASED ON A STORY BY | PADDY CHAYEFSKY |
| MUSIC BY | CYRIL MOCKRIDGE |
| DIRECTOR OF PHOTOGRAPHY | JOE MacDONALD, ASC |
| ART DIRECTION | LYLE WHEELER, MAURICE RANSFORD |
| FILM EDITOR | ROBERT SIMPSON |
| COSTUMES DESIGNED BY | RENIE |
| MUSICAL DIRECTION | LIONEL NEWMAN |

LENGTH 6,906 FEET
RUNNING TIME 1 HOUR
17 MINS

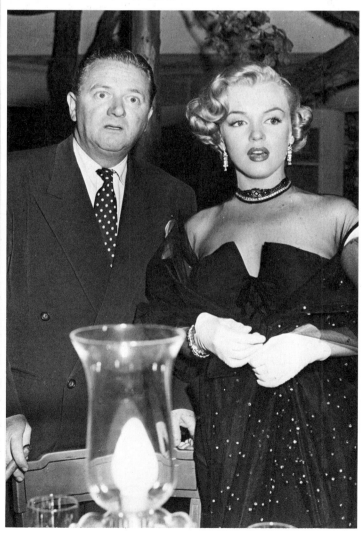

Wally Brown, Marilyn Monroe

# Love Nest

20th CENTURY FOX 15/10/1951

## CAST

| | |
|---|---|
| CONNIE SCOTT | JUNE HAVER |
| JIM SCOTT | WILLIAM LUNDIGAN |
| CHARLIE PATTERSON | FRANK FAY |
| ROBERTA STEVENS | MARILYN MONROE |
| ED FORBES | JACK PAAR |
| EADIE GAYNOR | LEATRICE JOY |
| GEORGE THOMPSON | HENRY KULKY |
| MRS QUIGG | MARIE BLAKE |
| FLORENCE | PATRICIA MILLER |
| MRS ARNOLD | MAUDE WALLACE |
| MR HANSEN | JOE PLOSKI |
| MRS THOMPSON | MARTHA WENTWORTH |
| MRS FRAZIER | FAIRE BINNEY |
| MRS McNAB | CARYL LINCOLN |
| MR McNAB | MICHAEL ROSS |
| MR FAIN | BOB JELLISON |
| POSTMAN | JOHN COSTELLO |
| MR KNOWLAND | CHARLES CALVERT |
| DETECTIVE DONOVAN | LEO CLARY |
| MR CLARK | JACK DALY |
| MR GRAY | RAY MONTGOMERY |
| MRS BRADDOCK | FLORENCE AUER |
| MRS ENGSTRAND | EDNA HOLLAND |
| MRS HEALY | LIZ SLIFER |
| GLAZIER | ALVIN HAMMER |

## CREDITS

| | |
|---|---|
| PRODUCED BY | JULES BUCK |
| DIRECTED BY | JOSEPH NEWMAN |
| SCREENPLAY BY | I A L DIAMOND |
| BASED ON A NOVEL BY | SCOTT CORBETT |
| MUSIC | CYRIL MOCKRIDGE |
| DIRECTOR OF PHOTOGRAPHY | LLOYD AHERN, ASC |
| ART DIRECTION | LYLE WHEELER |
| FILM EDITOR | J WATSON WEBB JR, ACE |
| COSTUMES DESIGNED BY | RENIE |
| MUSICAL DIRECTION | LIONEL NEWMAN |

LENGTH 7,509 FEET
RUNNING TIME 1 HOUR
24 MINS

C'MON 'A OUR HOUSE...
we'll give you lovin' ...laughin' and everything!
JUNE HAVER
WILLIAM LUNDIGAN
FRANK FAY
MARILYN MONROE
20th Century-Fox presents
LOVE NEST
SOON!......

# Let's Make it Legal

20th CENTURY FOX 23/10/1951

## CAST

| | |
|---|---|
| MIRIAM | CLAUDETTE COLBERT |
| HUGH | MacDONALD CAREY |
| VICTOR | ZACHARY SCOTT |
| BARBARA DENHAM | BARBARA BATES |
| JERRY DENHAM | ROBERT WAGNER |
| JOYCE | MARILYN MONROE |
| FERGUSON | FRANK CADY |
| GARDENER | JIM HAYWARD |
| MISS JESSUP | CAROL SAVAGE |
| MILKMAN | PAUL GERRITS |
| SECRETARY | BETTY JANE BOWEN |
| HUGH'S SECRETARY | VICI RAAF |
| POLICE LIEUTENANT | RALPH SANFORD |
| HOTEL MANAGER | HARRY DENNY |
| POSTMAN | HARRY HARVEY, SNR |

## CREDITS

| | |
|---|---|
| PRODUCED BY | ROBERT BASSLER |
| DIRECTED BY | RICHARD SALE |
| SCREENPLAY BY | F HUGH HERBERT |
| | I A L DIAMOND |
| BASED ON A STORY BY | MORTIMER BRAUS |
| MUSIC | CYRIL MOCKRIDGE |
| DIRECTOR OF PHOTOGRAPHY | LUCIEN BALLARD, ASC |
| ART DIRECTION | LYLE WHEELER, |
| | ALBERT HOGSETT |
| FILM EDITOR | ROBERT FRITCH, ACE |
| COSTUMES DESIGNED BY | RENIE |
| MUSICAL DIRECTION | LIONEL NEWMAN |

LENGTH 6,913 FEET
RUNNING TIME 1 HOUR
17 MINS

# Clash By Night

RKO 16/5/1952

## CAST

| | |
|---|---|
| MAE | BARBARA STANWYCK |
| JERRY | PAUL DOUGLAS |
| EARL | ROBERT RYAN |
| PEGGY | MARILYN MONROE |
| UNCLE VINCE | J CARROL NAISH |
| JOE DOYLE | KEITH ANDERS |
| PAPA | SILVIO MINCIOTTI |

## CREDITS

| | |
|---|---|
| DIRECTOR | FRITZ LANG |
| SCREENPLAY BY | ALFRED HAYES |
| FROM PLAY BY | CLIFFORD ODETS |
| PHOTOGRAPHY | NICHOLAS MUSURACA |
| MUSIC | ROY WEBB |
| EDITOR | GEORGE J AMY |
| SONG | 'I HEAR A RHAPSODY' |
| | SUNG BY TONY MARTIN |
| COSTUMES | MICHAEL WOULFE |

RUNNING TIME 105 MINS

# We're Not Married

20th CENTURY FOX 1/7/1952

## CAST

| | |
|---|---|
| RAMONA | GINGER ROGERS |
| STEVE GLADWYN | FRED ALLEN |
| JUSTICE OF THE PEACE | VICTOR MOORE |
| ANNABEL NORRIS | MARILYN MONROE |
| JEFF NORRIS | DAVID WAYNE |
| KATIE WOODRUFF | EVE ARDEN |
| HECTOR WOODRUFF | PAUL DOUGLAS |
| WILLIE FISHER | EDDIE BRACKEN |
| PATSY FISHER | MITZI GAYNOR |
| FREDDIE MELROSE | LOUIS CALHERN |
| EVE MELROSE | ZSA ZSA GABOR |
| DUFFY | JAMES GLEASON |
| ATTORNEY STONE | PAUL STEWART |
| MRS BUSH | JANE DARWELL |
| DETECTIVE MAGNUS | ALAN BRIDGE |
| RADIO ANNOUNCER | HARRY GOLDER |
| GOVERNOR BUSH | VICTOR SUTHERLAND |
| ATTORNEY GENERAL | TOM POWERS |
| ORGANIST | MAURICE CASS |
| AUTOGRAPH HOUND | MAUDE WALLACE |
| IRENE | MARGIE LISZT |
| MR GRAVES | RICHARD BUCKLEY |
| TWITCHELL | RALPH DUMKE |
| PINKY | LEE MARVIN |
| RUTHIE | MARJORIE WEAVER |
| POSTMAN | O Z WHITEHEAD |
| NED | HARRY HARVEY |
| CHAPLAIN HALL | SELMER JACKSON |

## CREDITS

| | |
|---|---|
| PRODUCED BY | NUNNALLY JOHNSON |
| DIRECTED BY | EDMUND GOULDING |
| SCREENPLAY BY | NUNNALLY JOHNSON |
| ADAPTED BY | DWIGHT TAYLOR |
| FROM A STORY BY | GINA KAUS, JAY DRATLER |
| MUSIC | CYRIL MOCKRIDGE |
| DIRECTOR OF PHOTOGRAPHY | LEO TOVER, ASC |
| ART DIRECTION | LYLE WHEELER, LELAND FULLER |
| FILM EDITOR | LOUIS LOEFFLER, ACE |
| COSTUMES DESIGNED BY | ELOIS JENSSEN |
| MUSICAL DIRECTION | LIONEL NEWMAN |

LENGTH 7,690 FEET
RUNNING TIME 1 HOUR
26 MINS

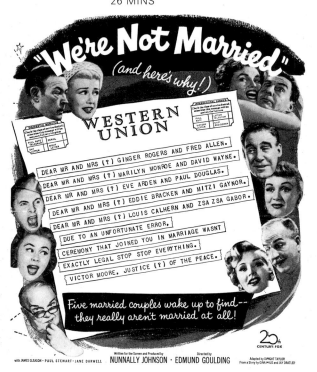

# Don't Bother to Knock

20th CENTURY FOX 17/7/1952

## CAST

| | |
|---|---|
| JED TOWERS | RICHARD WIDMARK |
| NELL | MARILYN MONROE |
| LYN LESLIE | ANNE BANCROFT |
| BUNNY | DONNA CORCORAN |
| ROCHELLE | JEANNE CAGNEY |
| MRS RUTH JONES | LURENE TUTTLE |
| EDDIE | ELISHA COOK JR |
| PETER JONES | JIM BACKUS |
| MRS BALLEW | VERNA FELTON |
| BARTENDER | WILLIS B BOUCHEY |
| MR BALLEW | DON BEDDOE |
| GIRL PHOTOGRAPHER | GLORIA BLONDELL |
| MRS McMURDOCK | GRACE HAYLE |
| PAT | MICHAEL ROSS |
| MAID | EDA REIS MERIN |
| LIFTMAN | VICTOR PERRIN |
| BELL CAPTAIN | DICK COGAN |
| DOORMAN | ROBERT FOULK |
| DESK CLERK | OLAN SOULE |
| TOASTMASTER | EMMETT VOGAN |

## CREDITS

| | |
|---|---|
| PRODUCED BY | JULIAN BLAUSTEIN |
| DIRECTED BY | ROY BAKER |
| SCREENPLAY BY | DANIEL TARADASH |
| BASED ON A NOVEL BY | CHARLOTTE ARMSTRONG |
| MUSICAL DIRECTION | LIONEL NEWMAN |
| DIRECTOR OF PHOTOGRAPHY | LUCIEN BALLARD, ASC |
| FILM EDITOR | GEORGE A GITTENS |
| COSTUMES DESIGNED BY | TRAVILLA |

LENGTH 6,846 FEET
RUNNING TIME 1 HOUR
16 MINS

Richard Widmark, Marilyn Monroe

# Monkey Business

### 20th CENTURY FOX 3/9/1952

## CAST

| | |
|---|---|
| BARNABY FULTON | CARY GRANT |
| EDWINA FULTON | GINGER ROGERS |
| MR OXLEY | CHARLES COBURN |
| LOIS LAUREL | MARILYN MONROE |
| HARVEY ENTWHISTLE | HUGH MARLOWE |
| SIEGFRIED KITZEL | HENRI LETONDAL |
| DR ZOLDECK | ROBERT CORNTHWAITE |
| MR CULVERLY | LARRY KEATING |
| MRS RHINELANDER | ESTHER DALE |
| LITTLE INDIAN | GEORGE WINSLOW |
| PAINTER | HEINE CONKLIN |
| YALE MAN | GIL STRATTON JR |
| REPORTER | HARRY CAREY JR |

## CREDITS

| | |
|---|---|
| DIRECTOR | HOWARD HAWKS |
| SCREENPLAY | BEN HECHT, CHARLES LEDERER, I A L DIAMOND |
| FROM STORY BY | HARRY SEGALL |
| PHOTOGRAPHY | MILTON KRASNER |
| EDITOR | WILLIAM B MURPHY |
| MUSIC | LEIGH HARLINE |
| COSTUMES | TRAVILLA |

RUNNING TIME 97 MINS

CARY GRANT
AND
MARILYN MONROE
IN A LITTLE BIT OF
"MONKEY BUSINESS"
THE FUNNIEST PICTURE
OF THE YEAR!

20th Century-Fox presents
CARY GRANT · GINGER ROGERS
CHARLES COBURN
MARILYN MONROE
in HOWARD HAWKS'
"MONKEY BUSINESS"

# O. Henry's Full House

### 20th CENTURY FOX 26/8/1952

5 short stories narrated by John
Steinbeck, Marilyn Monroe appeared in
the first of these
THE COP AND THE ANTHEM

## CAST

| | |
|---|---|
| SOAPY | CHARLES LAUGHTON |
| STREETWALKER | MARILYN MONROE |
| HORACE | DAVID WAYNE |

## CREDITS

| | |
|---|---|
| DIRECTOR | HENRY KOSTER |
| SCREENPLAY | LAMAR TROTTI |
| PHOTOGRAPHY | LLOYD AHERN |
| EDITOR | NICK DE MAGGIO |
| MUSIC | ALFRED NEWMAN |

RUNNING TIME 19 MINS

Titles of the other episodes:
The Clarion Call (Director: Henry Hathaway)
The Last Leaf (Director: Jean Negulesco)
The Ransom of the Red Chief (Director:
Howard Hawks)
The Gift of the Magi (Director: Henry King)

Marilyn Monroe, Charles Laughton

# Niagara

20th CENTURY FOX 22/1/1953

## CAST

| | |
|---|---|
| ROSE LOOMIS | MARILYN MONROE |
| GEORGE LOOMIS | JOSEPH COTTEN |
| POLLY CUTLER | JEAN PETERS |
| RAY CUTLER | CASEY ADAMS |
| INSPECTOR STARKEY | DENIS O'DEA |
| PATRICK | RICHARD ALLAN |
| MR KETTERING | DON WILSON |
| MRS KETTERING | LURENE TUTTLE |
| MR QUA | RUSSELL COLLINS |
| BOATMAN | WILL WRIGHT |
| DOCTOR | LESTER MATTHEWS |
| POLICEMAN | CARLETON YOUNG |
| SAM | SEAN McCLORY |
| LANDLADY | MINERVA URECAL |
| WIFE | NINI VARELA |
| HUSBAND | TOM REYNOLDS |
| STRAW BOSS | WINFIELD HOENY |
| CANADIAN CUSTOMS OFFICER | NEIL FITZGERALD |
| MORRIS | NORMAN McKAY |
| AMERICAN GUIDE | GENE BAXTER (WESSON) |
| CARILLON TOWER GUIDE | GEORGE IVES |
| DETECTIVE | PATRICK O'MOORE |

## CREDITS

| | |
|---|---|
| PRODUCED BY | CHARLES BRACKETT |
| DIRECTED BY | HENRY HATHAWAY |
| WRITTEN BY | CHARLES BRACKETT, WALTER REISCH AND RICHARD BREEN |
| MUSIC | SOL KAPLAN |
| DIRECTOR OF PHOTOGRAPHY | JOE MacDONALD, ASC |
| ART DIRECTION | LYLE WHEELER, MAURICE RANSFORD |
| FILM EDITOR | BARBARA McLEAN, ACE |
| COSTUMES DESIGNED BY | DOROTHY JEAKINS |
| SPECIAL PHOTOGRAPHIC EFFECTS | RAY KELLOGG |
| ASSISTANT DIRECTOR | GERD OSWALD |

RUNNING TIME 89 MINS

Marilyn Monroe, Joseph Cotton

# Gentlemen Prefer Blondes

20th CENTURY FOX 26/6/1953

## CAST

| | |
|---|---|
| DOROTHY | JANE RUSSELL |
| LORELEI | MARILYN MONROE |
| SIR FRANCIS BEEKMAN | CHARLES COBURN |
| MALONE | ELLIOT REID |
| GUS ESMOND | TOMMY NOONAN |
| HENRY SPOFFORD III | GEORGE WINSLOW |
| MAGISTRATE | MARCEL DALIO |
| ESMOND SR | TAYLOR HOLMES |
| LADY BEEKMAN | NORMA VARDEN |
| WATSON | HOWARD WENDELL |
| HOTEL MANAGER | STEVEN GERAY |
| GROTIER | HENRI LETONDAL |
| PHILLIPE | LEO MOSTOVOY |
| PRITCHARD | ALEX FRAZER |
| CAB DRIVER | GEORGE DAVIS |
| HEADWAITER | ALPHONSE MARTELL |
| COLOURED BOY DANCERS | JIMMIE & FREDDIE MOULTRIE |
| GENDARMES | JEAN DE BRIAC, GEORGE DEE, PETER CAMLIN |
| WINSLOW | HARRY CAREY JR |

## CREDITS

| | |
|---|---|
| PRODUCED BY | SOL C SIEGEL |
| DIRECTED BY | HOWARD HAWKS |
| SCREENPLAY BY | CHARLES LEDERER |
| BASED ON THE MUSICAL COMEDY BY | JOSEPH FIELDS & ANITA LOOS |
| MUSIC AND LYRICS BY | JULE STYNE & LEO ROBIN |
| MUSIC AND LYRICS | 'WHEN LOVE GOES WRONG' 'ANYONE HERE FOR LOVE?' BY HOAGY CARMICHAEL & HAROLD ADAMSON |
| CHOREOGRAPHY BY | JACK COLE |
| MUSICAL DIRECTION | LIONEL NEWMAN |
| DIRECTOR OF PHOTOGRAPHY | HARRY J WILD, ASC |
| ART DIRECTION | LYLE WHEELER, JOSEPH C WRIGHT |
| FILM EDITOR | HUGH S FOWLER |
| COSTUMES DESIGNED BY | TRAVILLA |
| VOCAL DIRECTION | ELIOT DANIEL |
| ORCHESTRATION | HERBERT SPENCER, EARLE HAGEN, BERNARD MAYERS |

RUNNING TIME 1 HOUR 25 MINS

Marilyn Monroe, Jane Russell, Elliot Reid

# How to Marry a Millionaire

20th CENTURY FOX 5/11/1953

## CAST

| | |
|---|---|
| LOCO | BETTY GRABLE |
| POLA | MARILYN MONROE |
| SCHATZE PAGE | LAUREN BACALL |
| FREDDIE DENMARK | DAVID WAYNE |
| EBEN | RORY CALHOUN |
| TOM BROOKMAN | CAMERON MITCHELL |
| J STEWARD MERRILL | ALEX D'ARCY |
| WALDO BREWSTER | FRED CLARK |
| J D HANLEY | WILLIAM POWELL |
| BENTON | PERCY HELTON |

## CREDITS

| | |
|---|---|
| PRODUCER | NUNNALLY JOHNSON |
| DIRECTOR | JEAN NEGULESCO |
| SCREENPLAY | NUNNALLY JOHNSON |
| BASED ON PLAYS BY | ZOE AKINS 'THE GREEKS HAD A WORD FOR IT'; DALE EUNSOR & KATHERINE ALBERT 'LOCO' |
| PHOTOGRAPHY (COLOUR) | JOE MacDONALD |
| EDITOR | LOUIS LOEFFLER |
| MUSICAL DIRECTION | ALFRED NEWMAN |
| INCIDENTAL MUSIC | CYRIL MOCKRIDGE |
| COSTUMES | TRAVILLA |

RUNNING TIME 95 MINS

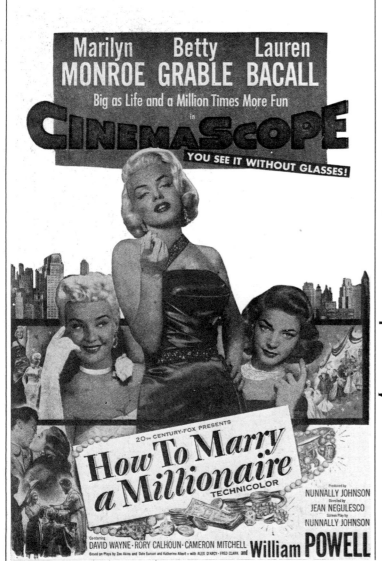

# River of No Return

20th CENTURY FOX 23/4/1954

## CAST

| | |
|---|---|
| MATT CALDER | ROBERT MITCHUM |
| KAY WESTON | MARILYN MONROE |
| HARRY WESTON | RORY CALHOUN |
| MARK | TOMMY RETTIG |
| COLBY | MURVYN VYE |
| BENSON | DOUGLAS SPENCER |
| GAMBLER | ED HINTON |
| BEN | DON BEDDOE |
| SURREY DRIVER | CLAIRE ANDRE |
| DEALER AT CRAP TABLE | JACK MATHER |
| BARBER | EDMUND COBB |
| TRADER | WILL WRIGHT |
| DANCER | JARMA LEWIS |
| YOUNG PUNK | HAL BAYLOR |

## CREDITS

| | |
|---|---|
| PRODUCED BY | STANLEY RUBIN |
| DIRECTED BY | OTTO PREMINGER |
| SCREENPLAY BY | FRANK FENTON |
| FROM A STORY BY | LOIUS LANTZ |
| COLOUR BY TECHNICOLOR | |
| MUSIC | CYRIL J MOCKRIDGE |
| MUSICAL DIRECTION | LIONEL NEWMAN |
| DIRECTOR OF PHOTOGRAPHY | JOSEPH LA SHELLE, ASC |
| ART DIRECTION | LYLE WHEELER, ADDISON HEHR |
| SPECIAL PHOTOGRAPHIC EFFECTS | RAY KELLOGG |
| WARDROBE DIRECTION | CHARLES LE MAIRE |
| COSTUMES DESIGNED BY | TRAVILLA |
| VOCAL DIRECTION | KEN DARBY |
| SONGS | 'THE RIVER OF NO RETURN' 'I'M GONNA FILE MY CLAIM' 'ONE SILVER DOLLAR' 'DOWN IN THE MEADOW' |
| LYRICS | KEN DARBY |
| MUSIC | LIONEL NEWMAN |
| CHOREOGRAPHY | JACK COLE |

RUNNING TIME 91 MINS

# There's No Business Like Show Business

20th CENTURY FOX 8/12/1954

## CAST

| | |
|---|---|
| MOLLY DONAHUE | ETHEL MERMAN |
| TIM DONAHUE | DONALD O'CONNOR |
| VICKY | MARILYN MONROE |
| TERRANCE DONAHUE | DAN DAILEY |
| STEVE DONAHUE | JOHNNIE RAY |
| KATY DONAHUE | MITZI GAYNOR |
| CHARLES GIBBS | HUGH O'BRIAN |
| EDDIE DUGGAN | FRANK McHUGH |
| FATHER DINEEN | RHYS WILLIAMS |
| MARGE | LEE PATRICK |
| STAGE MANAGER | LYLE TALBOT |
| LEW HARRIS | RICHARD EASTHAM |

## CREDITS

| | |
|---|---|
| DIRECTOR | WALTER LANG |
| SCREENPLAY | HENRY & PHECBE EPHRON |
| FROM A STORY BY | LAMARR TROTT |
| PHOTOGRAPHY | LEON SHAMROY |
| EDITOR | ROBERT SIMPSON |
| COSTUMES | MILES WHITE, |
| | BILLY TRAVILLA |
| CHOREOGRAPHY | ROBERT ALTON, JACK COLE |
| MUSIC | LIONEL ALFRED NEWMAN |
| ASSOCIATE | KEN DARBY |
| SONGS BY | IRVING BERLIN |

RUNNING TIME 117 MINS

Marilyn Monroe, Donald O'Connor, Mitzi Gaynor

# The Seven Year Itch

20th CENTURY FOX 3/6/1955

## CAST

| | |
|---|---|
| THE GIRL | MARILYN MONROE |
| RICHARD SHERMAN | TOM EWELL |
| HELEN SHERMAN | EVELYN KEYES |
| TOM McKENZIE | SONNY TUFTS |
| KRUHULIK | ROBERT STRAUSS |
| DR BRUBAKER | OSCAR HOMOLKA |
| MISS MORRIS | MARGUERITE CHAPMAN |
| PLUMBER | VICTOR MOORE |
| ELAINE | ROXANNE |
| MR BRADY | DONALD MacBRIDE |
| MISS FINCH | CAROLYN JONES |
| GIRL | DOROTHY FORD |
| RICKY SHERMAN | BUTCH BERNARD |
| WAITRESS | DORO MERANDO |

## CREDITS

| | |
|---|---|
| DIRECTOR | BILLY WILDER |
| SCREENPLAY | GEORGE AXELROD, |
| | BILLY WILDER |
| FROM THE STAGE PLAY BY | GEORGE AXELROD |
| PHOTOGRAPHY | MILTON S KRASNER |
| MUSIC | ALFRED NEWMAN |
| EDITOR | HUGH S FOWLER |
| COSTUMES | TRAVILLA |

RUNNING TIME 105 MINS

Marilyn Monroe, Tom Ewell

# Bus Stop

20th CENTURY FOX 15/8/1956

## CAST

| | |
|---|---|
| CHERIE | MARILYN MONROE |
| BO | DON MURRAY |
| VIRGIL | ARTHUR O'CONNELL |
| GRACE | BETTY FIELD |
| VERA | EILEEN HECKART |
| CARL | ROBERT PRAY |
| ELENA | HOPE LANGE |
| LIFE REPORTER | CASEY ADAMS |
| LIFE PHOTOGRAPHER | HANS CONREID |
| COVER GIRL | GRETA THYSSEN |

## CREDITS

| | |
|---|---|
| DIRECTOR | JOSHUA LOGAN |
| SCREENPLAY BY | GEORGE AXELROD |
| BASED ON THE PLAY | WILLIAM INGE |
| PHOTOGRAPHY (COLOUR) | MILTON KRASNER |
| EDITOR | WILLIAM REYNOLDS |
| MUSIC | ALFRED NEWMAN, CYRIL MOCKRIDGE |
| SONG | KEN DARBY |
| SUNG BY | THE FOUR LADS |
| COSTUMES | TRAVILLA |

RUNNING TIME 94 MINS

Marilyn Monroe, Don Murray

# The Prince and the Showgirl

WB 15/5/1957

## CAST

| | |
|---|---|
| THE REGENT | LAURENCE OLIVIER |
| ELSIE | MARILYN MONROE |
| THE QUEEN DOWAGER | SYBIL THORNDYKE |
| NORTHBROOK | RICHARD WATTIS |
| KING NICHOLAS | JEREMY SPENSER |
| HOFFMAN | ESMOND KNIGHT |
| MAJOR DOMO | PAUL HARDWICK |
| MAUD | ROSAMUND GREENWOOD |
| THE AMBASSADOR | AUBREY DEXTER |
| LADY SUNNINGDALE | MAXINE AUDLEY |
| CALL BOY | HAROLD GOODWIN |
| VALET WITH VIOLIN | ANDREA MELANDRINOS |
| MAISIE SPRINGFIELD | JEAN KENT |
| FANNY | DAPHNE ANDERSON |
| MAGGIE | GILLIAN OWEN |
| BETTY | VERA DAY |
| LOTTIE | MARGOT LISTER |
| THEATRE-MANAGER | CHARLES VICTOR |
| THE FOREIGN OFFICE | DAVID HORNE |
| HEAD VALET | DENNIS EDWARDS |
| DRESSER | GLADYS HENSON |

## CREDITS

| | |
|---|---|
| PRODUCER-DIRECTOR | LAURENCE OLIVIER |
| AUTHOR-SCRIPTWRITER | TERENCE RATTIGAN |
| ASSOCIATE DIRECTOR | ANTHONY BUSHELL |
| PRODUCTION DESIGNER | ROGER FURSE |
| ART DIRECTOR | CARMEN DILLON |
| DIRECTOR OF PHOTOGRAPHY | JACK CARDIFF |
| COSTUME DESIGNER | BEATRICE DAWSON |
| MUSIC COMPOSER | RICHARD ADDINSELL |
| MUSICAL DIRECTOR | MUIR MATHIESON |
| FILM EDITOR | JACK HARRIS |
| ASSISTANT EDITOR | DESMOND SAUNDERS |

RUNNING TIME 117 MINS

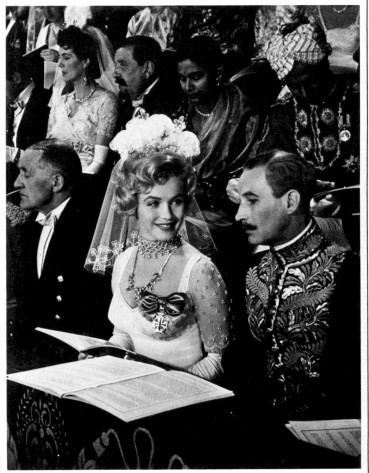

Marilyn Monroe, Richard Wattis

# Niagara

20th CENTURY FOX 22/1/1953

## CAST

| | |
|---|---|
| ROSE LOOMIS | MARILYN MONROE |
| GEORGE LOOMIS | JOSEPH COTTEN |
| POLLY CUTLER | JEAN PETERS |
| RAY CUTLER | CASEY ADAMS |
| INSPECTOR STARKEY | DENIS O'DEA |
| PATRICK | RICHARD ALLAN |
| MR KETTERING | DON WILSON |
| MRS KETTERING | LURENE TUTTLE |
| MR QUA | RUSSELL COLLINS |
| BOATMAN | WILL WRIGHT |
| DOCTOR | LESTER MATTHEWS |
| POLICEMAN | CARLETON YOUNG |
| SAM | SEAN McCLORY |
| LANDLADY | MINERVA URECAL |
| WIFE | NINI VARELA |
| HUSBAND | TOM REYNOLDS |
| STRAW BOSS | WINFIELD HOENY |
| CANADIAN CUSTOMS OFFICER | NEIL FITZGERALD |
| MORRIS | NORMAN McKAY |
| AMERICAN GUIDE | GENE BAXTER (WESSON) |
| CARILLON TOWER GUIDE | GEORGE IVES |
| DETECTIVE | PATRICK O'MOORE |

## CREDITS

| | |
|---|---|
| PRODUCED BY | CHARLES BRACKETT |
| DIRECTED BY | HENRY HATHAWAY |
| WRITTEN BY | CHARLES BRACKETT, WALTER REISCH AND RICHARD BREEN |
| MUSIC | SOL KAPLAN |
| DIRECTOR OF PHOTOGRAPHY | JOE MacDONALD, ASC |
| ART DIRECTION | LYLE WHEELER, MAURICE RANSFORD |
| FILM EDITOR | BARBARA McLEAN, ACE |
| COSTUMES DESIGNED BY | DOROTHY JEAKINS |
| SPECIAL PHOTOGRAPHIC EFFECTS | RAY KELLOGG |
| ASSISTANT DIRECTOR | GERD OSWALD |

RUNNING TIME 89 MINS

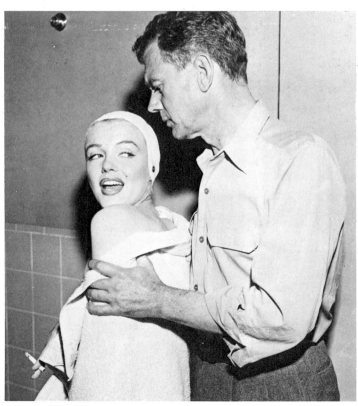

Marilyn Monroe, Joseph Cotton

# Gentlemen Prefer Blondes

20th CENTURY FOX 26/6/1953

## CAST

| | |
|---|---|
| DOROTHY | JANE RUSSELL |
| LORELEI | MARILYN MONROE |
| SIR FRANCIS BEEKMAN | CHARLES COBURN |
| MALONE | ELLIOT REID |
| GUS ESMOND | TOMMY NOONAN |
| HENRY SPOFFORD III | GEORGE WINSLOW |
| MAGISTRATE | MARCEL DALIO |
| ESMOND SR | TAYLOR HOLMES |
| LADY BEEKMAN | NORMA VARDEN |
| WATSON | HOWARD WENDELL |
| HOTEL MANAGER | STEVEN GERAY |
| GROTIER | HENRI LETONDAL |
| PHILLIPE | LEO MOSTOVOY |
| PRITCHARD | ALEX FRAZER |
| CAB DRIVER | GEORGE DAVIS |
| HEADWAITER | ALPHONSE MARTELL |
| COLOURED BOY DANCERS | JIMMIE & FREDDIE MOULTRIE |
| GENDARMES | JEAN DE BRIAC, GEORGE DEE, PETER CAMLIN |
| WINSLOW | HARRY CAREY JR |

## CREDITS

| | |
|---|---|
| PRODUCED BY | SOL C SIEGEL |
| DIRECTED BY | HOWARD HAWKS |
| SCREENPLAY BY | CHARLES LEDERER |
| BASED ON THE MUSICAL COMEDY BY | JOSEPH FIELDS & ANITA LOOS |
| MUSIC AND LYRICS BY | JULE STYNE & LEO ROBIN |
| MUSIC AND LYRICS | 'WHEN LOVE GOES WRONG' 'ANYONE HERE FOR LOVE?' BY HOAGY CARMICHAEL & HAROLD ADAMSON |
| CHOREOGRAPHY BY | JACK COLE |
| MUSICAL DIRECTION | LIONEL NEWMAN |
| DIRECTOR OF PHOTOGRAPHY | HARRY J WILD, ASC |
| ART DIRECTION | LYLE WHEELER, JOSEPH C WRIGHT |
| FILM EDITOR | HUGH S FOWLER |
| COSTUMES DESIGNED BY | TRAVILLA |
| VOCAL DIRECTION | ELIOT DANIEL |
| ORCHESTRATION | HERBERT SPENCER, EARLE HAGEN, BERNARD MAYERS |

RUNNING TIME 1 HOUR 25 MINS

Marilyn Monroe, Jane Russell, Elliot Reid

# How to Marry a Millionaire

20th CENTURY FOX 5/11/1953

## CAST

| | |
|---|---|
| LOCO | BETTY GRABLE |
| POLA | MARILYN MONROE |
| SCHATZE PAGE | LAUREN BACALL |
| FREDDIE DENMARK | DAVID WAYNE |
| EBEN | RORY CALHOUN |
| TOM BROOKMAN | CAMERON MITCHELL |
| J STEWARD MERRILL | ALEX D'ARCY |
| WALDO BREWSTER | FRED CLARK |
| J D HANLEY | WILLIAM POWELL |
| BENTON | PERCY HELTON |

## CREDITS

| | |
|---|---|
| PRODUCER | NUNNALLY JOHNSON |
| DIRECTOR | JEAN NEGULESCO |
| SCREENPLAY | NUNNALLY JOHNSON |
| BASED ON PLAYS BY | ZOE AKINS 'THE GREEKS HAD A WORD FOR IT'; DALE EUNSOR & KATHERINE ALBERT 'LOCO' |
| PHOTOGRAPHY (COLOUR) | JOE MacDONALD |
| EDITOR | LOUIS LOEFFLER |
| MUSICAL DIRECTION | ALFRED NEWMAN |
| INCIDENTAL MUSIC | CYRIL MOCKRIDGE |
| COSTUMES | TRAVILLA |

RUNNING TIME 95 MINS

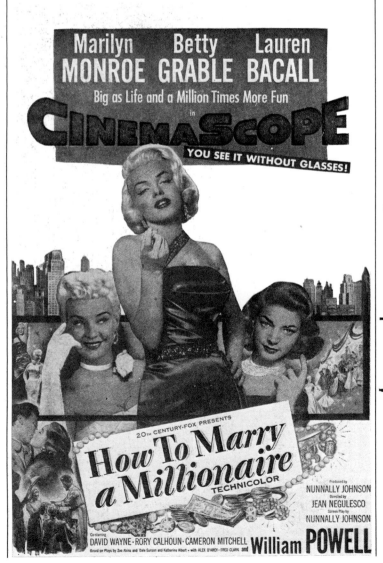

# River of No Return

20th CENTURY FOX 23/4/1954

## CAST

| | |
|---|---|
| MATT CALDER | ROBERT MITCHUM |
| KAY WESTON | MARILYN MONROE |
| HARRY WESTON | RORY CALHOUN |
| MARK | TOMMY RETTIG |
| COLBY | MURVYN VYE |
| BENSON | DOUGLAS SPENCER |
| GAMBLER | ED HINTON |
| BEN | DON BEDDOE |
| SURREY DRIVER | CLAIRE ANDRE |
| DEALER AT CRAP TABLE | JACK MATHER |
| BARBER | EDMUND COBB |
| TRADER | WILL WRIGHT |
| DANCER | JARMA LEWIS |
| YOUNG PUNK | HAL BAYLOR |

## CREDITS

| | |
|---|---|
| PRODUCED BY | STANLEY RUBIN |
| DIRECTED BY | OTTO PREMINGER |
| SCREENPLAY BY | FRANK FENTON |
| FROM A STORY BY | LOIUS LANTZ |
| COLOUR BY TECHNICOLOR | |
| MUSIC | CYRIL J MOCKRIDGE |
| MUSICAL DIRECTION | LIONEL NEWMAN |
| DIRECTOR OF PHOTOGRAPHY | JOSEPH LA SHELLE, ASC |
| ART DIRECTION | LYLE WHEELER, ADDISON HEHR |
| SPECIAL PHOTOGRAPHIC EFFECTS | RAY KELLOGG |
| WARDROBE DIRECTION | CHARLES LE MAIRE |
| COSTUMES DESIGNED BY | TRAVILLA |
| VOCAL DIRECTION | KEN DARBY |
| SONGS | 'THE RIVER OF NO RETURN' 'I'M GONNA FILE MY CLAIM' 'ONE SILVER DOLLAR' 'DOWN IN THE MEADOW' |
| LYRICS | KEN DARBY |
| MUSIC | LIONEL NEWMAN |
| CHOREOGRAPHY | JACK COLE |

RUNNING TIME 91 MINS

# Some Like It Hot

UA 25/2/1959

## CAST

| | |
|---|---|
| SUGAR | MARILYN MONROE |
| JOE | TONY CURTIS |
| JERRY | JACK LEMMON |
| SPATS | GEORGE RAFT |
| MULLIGAN | PAT O'BRIEN |
| OSGOOD | JOE E BROWN |
| BONAPARTE | NEHEMIAH PERSOFF |
| SUE | JOAN SHAWLEE |
| TOOTHPICK | GEORGE E STONE |
| PARADISE | EDWARD G ROBINSON |
| SPAT'S HENCHMEN | MIKE MAZURKI, HARRY WILSON |

## CREDITS

| | |
|---|---|
| PRODUCER AND DIRECTOR | BILLY WILDER |
| ASSOCIATE PRODUCERS | DOANE HARRISON, I A L DIAMOND |
| SCREENPLAY | BILLY WILDER, I A L DIAMOND |
| FROM A STORY BY | R THOEREN, M LOGAN |
| PHOTOGRAPHY | CHARLES LANG JR |
| MUSIC | ADOLPH DEUTSCH |
| EDITOR | ARTHUR SCHMIDT |
| COSTUMES | ORRY-KELLY |
| SONGS IN FILM INCLUDE | 'RUNNIN' WILD' 'I WANNA BE LOVED BY YOU' 'SWEET SUE' 'I'M THRU' WITH LOVE' 'BY THE BEAUTIFUL SEA' 'DOWN AMONG THE SHELTERING PALMS' |

RUNNING TIME 121 mins

# Let's Make Love

20th CENTURY FOX 24/8/1960

## CAST

| | |
|---|---|
| AMANDA | MARILYN MONROE |
| JEAN-MARC CLEMENT | YVES MONTAND |
| TONY DANTON | FRANKIE VAUGHAN |
| ALEXANDER COFFMAN | TONY RANDALL |
| JOHN WALES | WILFRED HYDE WHITE |
| OLIVER BURTON | DAVID BURNS |
| DAVE KERRY | MICHAEL DAVID |
| LILY NYLES | MARA LYNN |
| ABE MILLER | DENNIS KING JR |
| LAMONT | JOE BESSER |
| MISS MANNERS | MADGE KENNEDY |
| JIMMY | RAY FOSTER |
| YALE | MIKE MASON |
| COMSTOCK | JOHN CRAVEN |
| MINISTER | HARRY CHESHIRE |

## CREDITS

| | |
|---|---|
| PRODUCED BY | JERRY WALD |
| DIRECTED BY | GEORGE CUKOR |
| WRITTEN FOR THE SCREEN BY | NORMAN KRASNA |
| ADDITIONAL MATERIAL BY | HAL KANTER |
| MUSIC | LIONEL NEWMAN |
| WORDS AND MUSIC | SAMMY CAHN, JAMES VAN HEUSEN |
| SONG | 'MY HEART BELONGS TO DADDY' BY COLE PORTER |
| MUSICAL NUMBERS STAGED BY | JACK COLE |
| DIRECTOR OF PHOTOGRAPHY | DANIEL L FAPP, ASC |
| ART DIRECTION | LYLE R WHEELER |
| FILM EDITOR | DAVID BRETHERTON |
| COSTUMES DESIGNED BY | DOROTHY JEAKINS |

RUNNING TIME 118 mins

MARILYN MONROE and her bosom companions TONY CURTIS JACK LEMMON

IN A BILLY WILDER PRODUCTION "SOME LIKE IT HOT"

CO-STARRING GEORGE RAFT · PAT O'BRIEN · JOE E. BROWN

SCREEN PLAY BY BILLY WILDER and I.A.L. DIAMOND

DIRECTED BY BILLY WILDER

An ASHTON PICTURE · A Mirisch Company Presentation

RELEASED THRU UNITED ARTISTS

# The Misfits

UA 1/2/1961

## CAST

| | |
|---|---|
| GAY LANGLAND | CLARK GABLE |
| ROSLYN TABOR | MARILYN MONROE |
| PERCE HOWLAND | MONTGOMERY CLIFT |
| ISABELLE STEERS | THELMA RITTER |
| GUIDO | ELI WALLACH |
| THE OLD MAN IN THE BAR | JAMES BARTON |
| THE CHURCH LADY | ESTELLE WINWOOD |
| ROSLYN'S HUSBAND, RAYMOND TABER | KEVIN McCARTHY |
| YOUNG BOY IN BAR | DENNIS SHAW |
| CHARLES STEERS | PHILIP MITCHELL |
| OLD GROOM | WALTER RAMAGE |
| YOUNG BRIDE | PEGGY BARTON |
| FRESH COWBOY IN BAR | J LEWIS SMITH |
| SUSAN (AT R.R. STATION) | MARIETTA TREE |
| BARTENDER | BOBBY LaSALLE |
| MAN IN BAR | RYALL BOWKER |
| AMBULANCE ATTENDANT | RALPH ROBERTS |

## CREDITS

| | |
|---|---|
| PRODUCED BY | FRANK E TAYLOR |
| DIRECTED BY | JOHN HUSTON |
| SCREENPLAY BY | ARTHUR MILLER |
| MUSIC COMPOSED AND CONDUCTED BY | ALEX NORTH |
| DIRECTOR OF PHOTOGRAPHY | RUSSELL METTY, ASC |
| FILM EDITOR | GEORGE TOMASINI, ACE |
| MAIN TITLES | GEORGE NELSON & CO |
| COSTUMES | JEAN-LOUIS |

RUNNING TIME 2 HOURS
4 MINS

# Something's Got to Give

20th CENTURY FOX 1962

## CAST

MARILYN MONROE
DEAN MARTIN
CYD CHARISSE
PHIL SILVERS
WALLY COX

## CREDITS

| | |
|---|---|
| DIRECTOR | GEORGE CUKOR |
| SCREENPLAY | WALTER BERNSTEIN |
| ASSOCIATE PRODUCER & ART DIRECTOR | GENE ALLEN |
| PRODUCER | HENRY T. WEINSTEIN |
| PHOTOGRAPHY | FRANZ PLANER |
| COSTUMES | JEAN-LOUIS |

DUE TO MARILYN MONROE'S SUSPENSION AND SUBSEQUENT DEATH, THIS FILM WAS NEVER COMPLETED, AND WAS RE-SHOT WITH DORIS DAY, JAMES GARNER AND POLLY BERGEN IN THE ROLES ORIGINALLY INTENDED FOR MONROE, MARTIN AND CHARISSE IN WHAT WAS A REMAKE OF 'MY FAVOURITE WIFE', AND CALLED 'MOVE OVER DARLING' (1963)

# BIBLIOGRAPHY

Carpozi, George THE AGONY OF MARILYN MONROE *World Distributors, London, 1962.*

Conway, Michael, *and* Ricci, Mark THE FILMS OF MARILYN MONROE *Citadel Press, New York, 1964.*

Duran, Manuel VIDA Y MUERTE DE UN MITO *Universidad Nacional Autónoma de México, Mexico City. 1965. (Cuadernos de cine no. 13)*

Giglio, Tommaso MARILYN MONROE *Guanda, Bologna, 1956.*

Gilson, René MARILYN MONROE, 1926–1962 *Anthologie du Cinéma, Paris, 1969.*

Goode, James THE STORY OF *THE MISFITS Bobbs-Merrill, New York, 1963.*

Guiles, Fred Lawrence NORMA JEAN: THE LIFE OF MARILYN MONROE *McGraw-Hill Book Co., New York, 1969; W H Allen, London, 1969.*

Hoyt, Edwin P MARILYN: THE TRAGIC VENUS *Duell, Sloan & Pearce, New York, 1965.*

Kyrou, Ado MARILYN MONROE *Denoël, Paris, 1972. (Collection étoiles)*

Laclos, Michel MARILYN MONROE *Jean-Jacques Pauvert, Paris, 1963. (Vedettes du cinéma series)*

Madsen, Kai Berg EN AMERIKANSK SUKCES: HISTORIEN OM MARILYN MONROE *Illustrationsforlaget, Copenhagen, 1954.*

Mailer, Norman MARILYN: A BIOGRAPHY *Grosset & Dunlap Inc., New York, 1973; Hodder, London, 1973.*

Martin, Pete WILL ACTING SPOIL MARILYN MONROE? *Doubleday, New York, 1956.*

Smith, Milburn, *and others* MARILYN *Barven Publications, New York, 1971. (Screen Greats Series no. 4)*

Wagenknecht, Edward, *editor* MARILYN MONROE: A COMPOSITE VIEW *Chilton Book Company, Philadelphia, 1969.*

Zolotow, Maurice MARILYN MONROE *W H Allen, London, 1961.*

Axelrod, George & Shaw, Sam MARILYN MONROE AS THE GIRL: The Making of *The Seven Year Itch* in Pictures by Sam Shaw; Foreword by George Axelrod. *Ballantine Books New York, 1955.*

Hamblett, Charles WHO KILLED MARILYN MONROE? or Cage to Catch our Dreams. *Leslie Frewin Ltd., London, 1966.*

Bessie, Alvah THE SYMBOL: a novel whose main heroine bears close study and gives a more penetrating insight into a girl like Marilyn than is usually allowed a biographer. *The Bodley Head, Ltd., London, 1966.*

Miller, Arthur AFTER THE FALL: a play by Monroe's ex-husband whose central character is a self destructive movie star. *Viking Press, New York, 1961.*

Miller, Arthur THE MISFITS: a synthesis of screenplay and novel, including the original short story first published in ESQUIRE which Miller turned into a highly personal movie for his wife, and which he dedicated to Clark Gable. *Dell Publishing Co. Inc. New York, 1957, 1961.*

# DISCOGRAPHY

LET'S MAKE LOVE Philips BBL 7414/SBBL 592 (1960). US Columbia CL-1527/CS-8327 (1960).

SOME LIKE IT HOT US United Artists UAL 4030/UAS-5030 (1959). US Ascot UM-13500/US-16500 (1964).

GENTLEMEN PREFER BLONDES (with Jane Russell) US MGM E-208 (10") (1953). Re-issued with 'Till the Clouds Roll By', MGM 2353 067 Select.

THE MISFITS US United Artists UAL-4087/UAS-5087 (1965).

THE SEVEN YEAR ITCH US Decca 8123/8312. Mercury 20154.

MARILYN MONROE Music for Pleasure MFP 1176 (1963). Sound track of film *Marilyn.* Contents: 3 songs *There's No Business Like Show Business* 4 songs *River of No Return* 4 songs *Gentlemen Prefer Blondes* (without Jane Russell)

HOW TO MARRY A MILLIONAIRE One of the tracks on Captain from Castile: classic film scores of Alfred Newman. RCA ARLI 0184 (1973).

# INDEX

# Acknowledgements

For once there is not a long list of family friends and passers-by to thank for their help in making this book possible. The book was a joy to do because the few who were involved in it shared my feeling for the subject and contributed enormously with their talents and enthusiasm. So thanks, Janice Anderson and Peter Arnold. Thanks, too, Joel Coler at 20th Century Fox for additional stills, and thanks Jeff Fairman for helping so generously. Robin Dodd designed the book so that pictures could say what words failed to, and David Robinson wrote his text with affection and insight, and a beauty which matched his subject. For permission to reproduce the stills in this book I wish to thank the companies that made the films that starred Marilyn Monroe: United Artists, RKO, MGM, Warner Brothers and, of course, 20th Century Fox. I also thank Camera Press, who provided the pictures on pages 144 and 145. The Time and Life covers on page 35 are reproduced by permission of Life Magazine and Time, The Weekly News Magazine, © Time Inc, 1973. The Paris-Match and Neue Illustrierte covers on the same page are reproduced by permission of the publishers.